WILLIAM T.
SHERMAN

Great American Generals

WILLIAM T.

SHERMAN

Marsha Landreth

GALLERY BOOKS
An imprint of W.H. Smith Publishers Inc.
112 Madison Avenue
New York, New York 10016

Published by Gallery Books
A Division of W H Smith Publishers Inc.
112 Madison Avenue
New York, New York 10016

Produced by
Brompton Books Corp.
15 Sherwood Place
Greenwich, CT 06830

ISBN 0-8317-4077-9

Printed in Hong Kong

10 9 8 7 6 5 4 3 2 1

PICTURE CREDITS

Brompton Photo Library: 1, 2(both), 22, 23(bottom right), 27,
    33(top), 34-35(both), 49, 59(bottom), 63(bottom), 67(both), 71.
Anne S.K. Brown Military Collection, Brown University: 9, 18, 19,
    20(bottom), 23(top left), 25(bottom left), 26(top), 32-33, 41,
    43(bottom), 46, 53(top), 60.
Chicago Historical Society: 8(left), 15(bottom), 28(left), 36(left),
    44-45.
Library of Congress: 7, 8(right), 10(bottom), 15(top), 17(both),
    20(top), 29, 30(bottom), 36(right), 37, 40(top), 42-43(top),
    48(left), 50-51, 52-53(bottom), 53(bottom), 54(both), 59(top),
    61(bottom), 62, 63(top), 64-65(all three), 69, 73, 74-75(both), 76,
    77(left), 78.
Mansell Collection: 48(right).
Museum of the Confederacy: 24.
National Archives: 4-5, 6(left), 13, 16, 21(top), 25(top right), 38-39,
    40(bottom), 47(both), 55(both), 56-57, 58, 61(top), 70, 72.
National Portrait Gallery, Smithsonian Institution: 10(top), 11.
Richard Natkiel: 26(bottom), 31, 66.
Naval Academy Museum, Beverly R. Robinson Collection: 30(top).
Peter Newark's Western Americana: 3, 14, 79.
New York Public Library, Prints Division: 12.
Norfolk Southern Corporation: 68(top).
Smithsonian Institution, National Anthropological Archives:
    6(right).
Sutro Library: 77(right).
U.S. Naval Historical Center Photograph: 68(bottom).
V M I Museum: 21(bottom).
Louis A. Warren Lincoln Library and Museum, Fort Wayne, IN:
    28(right).

ACKNOWLEDGMENTS

The publisher would like to thank the following people who helped
in the preparation of this book: Don Longabucco, who designed it;
Rita Longabucco, who did the picture research; and John Kirk,
who edited the text.

Page 1: *Members of a Union Army band at the front.*

Page 2: *Scenes from two of Sherman's most noteworthy campaigns. Above, the Battle of Kennesaw Mountain, fought during the march on Atlanta. Below, an incident during the Siege of Vicksburg.*

Page 3: *The fierce, driven quality we associate with Sherman's strange character is well captured in this old engraving of the general.*

Pages 4-5: *Confederate guns and fortifications outside Atlanta, photographed after Sherman took the city.*

Contents

Early Years

On February 8, 1820, in Lancaster, Ohio, Charles Sherman's wife presented him with the opportunity for which he had waited nearly eight years. The lawyer, a great admirer of Tecumseh, had decided to name his next son after the Shawnee Indian chief. Because his first born, Charles, had been named after one of his wife's two brothers, Mary Sherman insisted on naming the next son after her other brother. Mrs. Sherman was out of brothers, so Charles could now have his Tecumseh (meaning "shooting star"). But his wait was not over. Not only was the second baby a girl, the fourth and fifth were also girls. But finally, on that cold winter day the red-haired boy came screaming into the world, and Sherman at last had his Shooting Star.

"Cump" (Tecumseh was more than a mouthful for his three sisters and two brothers) was followed by five more siblings before his father suddenly died, apparently from typhoid fever, while riding the court circuit as judge. When Judge Sherman's colleague, friend and neighbor, Thomas Ewing, discovered that his friend's widow would have to provide for her large family on only a small legacy from her father, Ewing took up a collection, paid off the mortgage and took in one of the children.

So it was that the nine-year-old Cump put his little hand in one of Ewing's big ones and walked up the hill to the larger house next door. Yet the transition was smooth, since the boy had spent much of his time in the Ewing home playing with his friend Philemon Ewing. And in any case, Philemon and Cump, with hangers-on Eleanor, called Ellen (five), and little Hugh (two), could always wander in and out of the Sherman home and play with Cump's brothers and sisters.

The boy was still a Sherman, and Thomas Ewing would not have dreamed of taking that legacy from his friend's child by adopting him, but he did allow another name change. Ewing, like the Shermans, was a Protestant, but his wife was a staunch Catholic. When it was discovered that Cump had somehow missed being baptized, Maria Ewing ran next door to ask Mary Sherman if the visiting priest could perform the ceremony. Mary had no objections. The priest, upon learning the boy's name, insisted that he be named for a saint, and because that day was the feast of St. William, the child was christened William.

As William Tecumseh Sherman grew, one by one his brothers and sisters moved away, taken in by friends and relatives. As a result, his ties became ever stronger with the Ewing clan. Thomas Ewing kept a careful eye on the boy's education, even when his duties as United States senator demanded his absence. As a senator, Ewing was given the power to appoint each year one young man from his district to West Point, and he had already appointed one of his wife's relatives, William Irving, in 1835. In 1836 he had to

Below: *Photographic portrait of William Tecumseh Sherman as a young army officer.*

Below right: *Tecumseh, the great Shawnee chief for whom Sherman was named.*

choose between his son Philemon and Cump. He chose Cump.

The 16-year-old packed his belongings and headed to West Point by way of Washington. The stage took him as far as Frederick; from there he had to make a choice between going by train or two-horse hack. "Not having full faith in the novel and dangerous railroad, I stuck to the coach." No doubt he chuckled as he wrote this in his memoirs long after the Civil War, knowing how important the railroads had been to him in moving men and supplies.

After a visit with his foster father in Washington, where he got his first glimpse of the federal government in action, Cump proceeded north. West Point did little to enhance his self-esteem. The tall, thin boy found himself surrounded by Southerners, all of whom were better riders and swordsmen and who possessed greater confidence and finer manners. Only academically was Sherman their superior.

General Sherman would write in his memoirs: "At the Academy I was not considered a good soldier, for at no time was I selected for any office, but remained a private throughout the whole four years . . . My average demerits, per annum, were about one hundred and fifty, which reduced my final class standing from number four to six."

Young Sherman did, however, make a number of friends

US Marines moving against Indians in the Seminole Wars, Lieutenant Sherman saw almost no fighting, but the action was his first exposure to the institution of slavery.

at the Academy, among them classmates, Stewart Van Vliet and George H. Thomas. He also had the opportunity to observe other cadets who would later play important parts in his life, future commanders such as Braxton Bragg, Joseph Hooker, Pierre Gustave Toutant Beauregard and Henry Halleck. In his fourth year another Ohioan came to West Point: Hiram Ulysses Grant. The boy insisted that the name on the roll, Ulysses S. Grant, was wrong and wanted it corrected, but he was told that until orders to the contrary were received the name would remain as written, and so it did, to the end of his life.

In the four years at West Point Sherman grew from boy to man, and one symptom of his new maturity was his desire for financial independence. To his mother he confided, "I do not wish to ever ask Mr. Ewing again for assistance." His goal of independence might have been more easily realized if Mr. Ewing had remained in his role as foster father instead of becoming his father-in-law.

Above: *Major Robert Anderson, the commander of Fort Sumter. The news of his surrender to the Confederates on April 13, 1861, electrified Sherman, who quickly accepted a posting as colonel in the US Infantry.*

Above: *Slaves picking cotton on a Southern plantation. Sherman had no exposure to the institution of slavery until his transfer to Florida as a second lieutenant in the Seminole Wars.*

Sherman was not the only one in the Ewing family to blossom into adulthood. Ellen, Cump's faithful correspondent, was 16 in 1840 when the newly-commissioned lieutenant joined the Third Artillery on the east coast of Florida at Fort Pierce. To the 20-year-old officer Ellen was still little more than a beloved sister, but that would change.

Although the young lieutenant saw practically no action in the war against the Seminole Indians, he did encounter slavery for the first time. In an attempt to return runaway slaves who found refuge among the Seminoles, the government had been battling the Indians intermittently since 1821. Thus Sherman was introduced to slavery as an institution his government was defending.

By the time Sherman came to the Seminole Wars their character had changed. The massacres and battles of past years had now been replaced by deliberate destruction of the Indians' homes and crops in an attempt to break their morale. It was a cruelly effective policy, and one that the young officer would long remember.

After only 18 months Sherman was promoted to the rank of first lieutenant and transferred to a post close to St.

Augustine, Florida, where fellow West Pointer Lt. Braxton Bragg was also stationed. Sherman found that he enjoyed Southern society, and in one of his letters to Ellen he commented on the beauty of the Spanish girls. In Ellen's next letter she suggested that he leave the army.

Shortly afterward the whole regiment was transferred to Fort Moultrie near Charleston, South Carolina. His next five years at Fort Moultrie allowed a good deal of leisure time. Sherman was entertained in hospitable homes by articulate gentlemen and gracious ladies, and he roamed the countryside, took up painting and became infatuated with the South. He still found no quarrel with slavery.

Though Sherman loved painting, he feared his passion might become all-consuming, and he put away his paints permanently after a three-month furlough home in the summer of 1843. Ellen was now 19, and before he returned to duty they may have become engaged, though this is not absolutely clear. The uncertainties about this 1843 engagement stem from a possibly apocryphal story that has Sherman involved in a Southern romance in 1844. The need to take a deposition had given him an opportunity to visit a West Point classmate in 1844, as well as the opportunity to travel over the land on which he would later fight. Apparently he was so taken with his friend's sister that he proposed, but, as the story goes, he was turned down because he had cruel eyes. He protested to no avail and ended by saying that he would always protect her. Twenty years later he would be true to his word: her house would stand undisturbed along the burnt path left by Sherman's army.

For a time during his stint at Fort Moultrie, Sherman and his close friend Captain Robert Anderson amused themselves by watching the army engineers build a new fort, to be named Sumter, on a man-made island. But soon the war with Mexico was at hand, and his group of friends scattered. Sherman yearned to go to Mexico, but he received orders instead to report to Ohio as a recruiter.

His one chance to see action came when, hearing of the victories at Palo Alto and Resaca de la Palma, Sherman personally escorted 30 recruits to Newport, Kentucky, and then went on to Cincinnati to volunteer for service in Mexico. The colonel of the Western recruiting service was not receptive, and his hopes of being ordered into action were dashed. Said Sherman, "Instead of appreciating my volunteer zeal, he cursed and swore at me for leaving my post without orders, and told me to go back to Pittsburg."

New orders greeted him upon his return. He hurriedly completed his reports and wrote a note to Ellen, 36 miles away, then rushed to New York, where he barely caught his ship, the *Lexington*. With his roommate, Lt. Edward Ord, and Lt. Halleck, Cump sailed around Cape Horn, landing in Monterey Bay, California, 198 days later. Alas, Sherman did not find glory in California either. During his three-year stay there he saw no action whatever, but at least he did strengthen his skills as quartermaster, skills that would serve him well during the Civil War.

He made the first of many financial mistakes when, unlike Halleck and many of his other friends, he declined to buy a lot in San Francisco for $16. After gold fever hit California, Sherman found that "any room twenty-by-sixty feet would rent for $1000 a month." His army pay remained $70 a month at a time when "no one would even try to hire a servant under three hundred dollars."

Sherman had actually been one of the first to hear of the gold discovery, having been handed a letter from Captain Sutter in the spring of 1848 that requested "preemption" of the land around Sutter's saw mill. Sherman would write in his memoirs that he replied "that California was yet a Mexican province, simply held by us as a conquest; that no laws of the United States yet applied to it, much less the land laws or preemption laws, which could only apply after a public survey. Therefore it was impossible for the Governor to promise him a title to the land; yet, as there were no settlements within forty miles, he was not likely to be disturbed by trespassers." It never seems to have occured to the honorable Sherman that the information in Sutter's letter could have been used for Sherman's personal profit.

Orders at last arrived for Sherman to return to the east coast. No doubt Thomas Ewing, now secretary of the interior in President Taylor's cabinet, was responsible for Sherman's assignment to Washington, and Cump was greeted warmly by his Ewing family, who now lived in a rented mansion on Pennsylvania Avenue. Ellen, having waited faithfully all these years, was fast approaching old-maid status at 26, and the Ewings were ready for a wedding. It duly took place on May Day, 1850.

Sherman's next post was in St. Louis. Preparing for the

The capture of Mexican General La Vega at the battle of Resaca de la Palma on May 9, 1846. Hearing of such US victories in the Mexican War, Lieutenant Sherman left his post at Fort Moultrie, South Carolina, to go to Cincinnati to volunteer for service in Mexico.

Right: *A portrait of the Seminole leader Osceola by the artist George Catlin. Osceola's refusal to migrate west touched off the Second Seminole War.*

Right below: *A recruiting poster seeking volunteers to form a cavalry regiment for duty in the Mexican War. Sherman was stationed in California, where he saw no fighting.*

Opposite: *An 1863 portrait of General Henry W. Halleck. A friend of Sherman's from their early days together at West Point and in California, Halleck recognized Sherman's talent for military planning.*

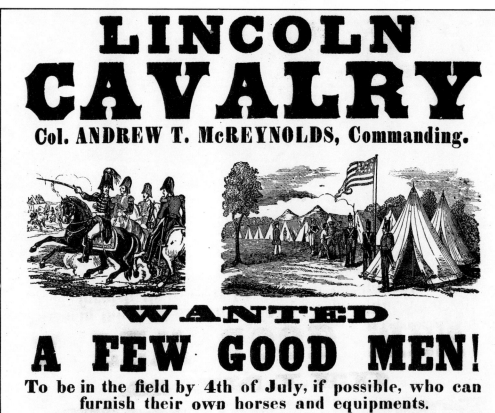

birth of the first Sherman child, Ellen left on one of her many visits to Lancaster, Ohio, to which the Ewings had returned after Thomas resigned from the cabinet after President Fillmore took office. Cump reverted to his bachelor lifestyle, spending pleasant hours with Bragg and Van Vliet.

But despite all this, Sherman was strangely unhappy. This despondency may have stemmed from worrying that he could not provide for Ellen in the manner to which she was accustomed, or perhaps, as he wrote to Ellen, it was that "I am getting tired of this dull, tame life and should a fair opportunity occur for another campaign on the frontier, I

cannot promise to keep quiet. Commissaries are not fighting men." Possibly there was no rational cause at all for his depression. But whatever it might have been, Sherman left the army, after 17 years, to become the manager of the San Francisco branch of a St. Louis bank.

The cold and fog of the San Francisco winters played havoc with Cump's asthma, but he endured the weather long enough to straighten out the bank's affairs after the financial crash that hit the city in 1855. Although his bank did not, thanks to Sherman's foresight, suffer great losses, he did lose a good deal of the money he had invested for

several of his army comrades, including Bragg. Over the next few years he would personally repay all investors, even though the losses had not been his fault. It was a matter of honor.

In 1857 Sherman closed the San Francisco branch and was transferred to the New York office. The depression followed him to New York, and soon that bank, too, closed its doors. He hurried back to St. Louis with all the bank's assets.

St. Louis at this time hosted not only the disheartened Sherman but another West Pointer, Ulysses S. Grant. Grant was now working his wife's farm and occasionally peddled firewood on the city streets. Neither man had fared well in the peace-time army or in civilian life.

After settling the bank's accounts, and to Ellen's great joy, Sherman was tempted to accept Thomas Ewing's standing offer to work in Ohio superintending the family's saltworks. By accepting the offer he felt he was giving up any hope of regaining his self-respect, yet for the sake of his ever-increasing family he felt he must do it. But in the end he wrote Ewing: "You can understand what Ellen does not, that a man needs a consciousness of position and influence among his peers. In the Army I know my place, and out here

Above: *A lithograph of San Francisco at the middle of the nineteenth century. Here Sherman represented a St. Louis banking firm for a period of three years.*

Right: *A painting of Sherman as he appeared in 1860 after his appointment as the first superintendent of the new Louisiana State Military Academy.*

am one of the Pioneers . . . at Lancaster I can only be Cump Sherman."

So, instead of going to the saltworks, Sherman accepted the younger Tom Ewing's offer to join his law firm in Leavenworth. He was admitted to the bar on his general knowledge, but he soon found that he was too "red-headed" to tolerate courtroom decorum. Then, on January 1, 1860, with help from Braxton Bragg and Pierre Beauregard, Sherman was appointed the first superintendent of the newly formed Louisiana State Military Academy (later to become Louisiana State University.) After seven years of frustration and bitter failures, Sherman seemed finally to have found his niche in civilian life.

Secession to Bull Run

Lincoln's election in November, 1860, brought to a climax the bitter dispute between the North and South over states rights and slavery. A month later South Carolina seceded; within six weeks Mississippi, Florida, Alabama, Georgia, Louisiana and Texas followed. By February the new nation, the Confederate States of America, had elected Jefferson Davis its president. On June 8, 1861, Tenessee would be the 11th and final state to secede.

With the news of South Carolina's secession in December, Sherman made several prophetic remarks to one of the professors, whom he would later retrieve from a prison camp. In essence, they all added up to, "Boyd, you people of the south don't know what you are doing." The intense Sherman insisted that there would be bloodshed and that the South was doomed to fail. Not only because the 22 states that had rallied to the Northern cause had a population of 22 million to the Confederate States' 9 million, but also because the North had 92 percent of the nation's industry. But Boyd was doubtless just the sounding board for Sherman's frustration. Sherman knew that if Louisiana seceded he would be honor-bound to give up his position and move north. Although he had no particular quarrel with slavery and held great affection for the South, he knew that his keen belief in federalism, instilled by his foster father, would ultimately define his loyalties.

Sherman anguished over the plight of his old friend Major Robert Anderson, commandant of Fort Sumter, as the Confederates surrounded the fort during January, 1861. With Louisiana's secession on January 26, 1861, Sherman tendered his resignation at LSMA and traveled to New Orleans to transfer the school's funds to the board of directors. During his stay in the city he met with his friends Bragg

Right: *President Abraham Lincoln during his first term in office. Although he had presented himself as a moderate, his election reinforced the determination of some Southern states to secede from the Union.*

Above: *Abraham Lincoln's first inauguration, May 4, 1861, on the steps of the US capitol. By this time Jefferson Davis had already been inaugurated president of the Confederate States of America. With the South's secession, Sherman resigned his position at Louisiana State Military Academy.*

Left: *A lithograph "Come and Join Us Brothers" published by the Supervisory Committee for Recruiting Colored Regiments in Philadelphia. Almost 200,000 blacks served in both armies, and some 2500 were killed in action.*

Opposite: *Munitions lined up at a wharf in Yorktown, Virginia, for transport to Union General McClellan's forces in the Peninsula. Sherman knew that Northern manufacturing superiority would be crucial in the coming war.*

Left: *On November 7, 1860,* Harper's Weekly *published this jibe at the pre-war volunteer movement in the North.*

and Beauregard, though the visit with Beauregard was short, for Jefferson Davis had already sent for him. After receiving an appointment as brigadier general, Beauregard was to take command of the Southern forces in Charleston. Sherman's friends Beauregard and Anderson would thus soon be pitted against each other.

From Louisiana, Sherman traveled to Lancaster, Ohio, where he found an invitation to visit his brother John, now a senator, in Washington. Accordingly, he stopped off at Washington on his way to St. Louis, where he had been offered a position as president of the Fifth Street Railroad. In Washington, Senator Sherman took his brother to see the new president of the United States, Abraham Lincoln.

To Lincoln John said, "Mr. President, this is my brother, Colonel Sherman, who is just up from Louisiana; he may give you some information you want." Lincoln replied, "Ah! how are they getting along down there?" Sherman answered, "They think they are getting along swimmingly – they are preparing for war." Lincoln said, "Oh, well! I guess we'll manage to keep house." Sherman was thunderstruck; even the president did not seem to understand what was

happening. On the street he lashed out at his brother, saying that the politicians "got things in a hell of a fix, and you may get them out as you best can."

The fall of Fort Sumter on April 13, 1861, prompted Lincoln to issue a call for 75,000 volunteers to serve for three months. Those months rapidly vanished in a welter of administrative, organizational and logistical problems. Adding to the problems of feeding, clothing and training this amateur army was the frustration of knowing that from his White House windows the president could see Beauregard's Confederate camp across the Potomac.

Sherman quickly declined a Confederate command and then a position as the Union's assistant Secretary of War. Although he volunteered for Union service, he declined a political appointment as brigadier-general because he did not want to be indebted to politicians. When, on May 14, 1861, he was offered an appointment as a colonel of the Thirteenth Regular Infantry, he jumped at it.

Sherman's newly created regiment was made up of volunteers from New York and Wisconsin, men who in many cases had never even seen a musket before, let alone

Left: *The firing on Fort Sumter in Charleston Harbor in April, 1861, caused Sherman considerable anxiety over the plight of its commander, his old friend Major Robert Anderson. Anderson was later promoted to brigadier general.*

The Confederate Black Horse Cavalry falls to an attack by Union Zouaves at the First Battle of Bull Run. The colorful but impractical uniforms of the Zouaves were patterned after those of Algerian units in the French army. Both sides fielded brightly uniformed troops in the war.

fired one. The commissioned officers and noncoms were not much better. It was Sherman and his handful of regulars who trained the raw recruits.

Under constant pressure from politicians to take Richmond, the Confederate capital, the Union Army under General Irvin McDowell started its advance on July 16, 1861. Of the march through the Virginia countryside Sherman wrote: "The march demonstrated little save the general laxity of discipline; for with all my personal efforts I could not prevent the men from straggling for water, blackberries, or anything on the way they fancied."

McDowell, on the eve of battle, called a war council in his rustic Centreville headquarters. Sherman arrived early and, using McDowell's table, wrote Ellen a light-hearted letter, just in case it was his last. McDowell then spread a map over the earth floor. He told General Daniel Tyler – Sherman's commander – to hold the lower fords of Bull Run; Colonel Dixon Miles would be held at Centreville in reserve, and General David Hunter would spearhead the main attack by Warrenton Turnpike. General S. P. Heintzelman would then follow Hunter. Tyler argued that the confrontation should be cancelled because, having all day long heard trains pulling into Manassas Junction, a few miles south, he feared correctly that P. G. T. Beauregard's troops were being reinforced by General Joseph E. Johnston. But McDowell was determined: he knew that the 90-day enlistments would

soon expire, making another timely advance impossible. So on July 21, 1861, his army, some 35,000 strong, attacked the Confederates at Bull Run in what Sherman termed "one of the best-planned battles of the war, but one of the worst-fought."

At 6:30 in the morning, when the warm summer sun was almost two hours old, General Tyler's division was in position at Stone Bridge to act as decoy and guard against a counterattack while the main assault crossed Bull Run Creek near Sudley Church, wide of the Confederate left flank. Sherman's part in the battle was to fire cannons now and again to draw attention away from Hunter's and Heintzelman's troops. Finding that his smooth-bore guns did not reach the enemy's position, Sherman sent word to Tyler asking for the three-ton thirty-pounder cannon, and thereafter Sherman and his men lobbed an occasional ball across the creek and waited in the hot fields north of Bull Run for three hours until finally sounds of battle roared in the distance. Hunter and Heintzelman had been delayed, in part due to the road being blocked by backed-up regiments of Tyler's division.

But the demonstration near Stone Bridge did not fool Confederate brigade commander N. G. Evans, who quickly shifted his forces toward the main attack near Warrenton Turnpike. At noon, according to Sherman's report, the sounds of artillery across Bull Run revealed that the main assault was stalled.

By now Tyler had received a message from McDowell to press the attack, so he ordered Sherman to cross the creek and support McDowell's forces. This was no problem, since Sherman, having earlier watched a Confederate horseman ford Bull Run, knew that where one soldier could cross, so could a brigade of 3400. On the other side of the creek Sherman hurried through the woods and the field of death-blackened bodies, but he slowed as he approached the battle site. One of his regiments had two companies dressed in gray uniforms, and he feared they might be mistaken for the enemy. As it turned out, it was General Barnard Bee's Confederate troops who saw them first, and, thinking the men in gray were reinforcements, the Confederates moved to reform their line behind the arriving unit. The new unit, however, opened fire, seriously wounding the Confederate regiment's last two field officers, and without a leader the Confederate troops faltered. Soon Sherman was joined by Tyler, who came over with Erasmus Keyes' brigade, and then Heintzelman arrived with a battery of six ten-pounder guns. The Confederates were driven back as far as Henry House Hill, high ground overlooking Warrenton Turnpike where it intersected the Manassas-Sudley Road.

Confederate Brigadier General Thomas J. Jackson waited on Henry House Hill with his well-placed men. He had just arrived by train, had followed the sounds of battle and was now carefully deploying his men in a shallow depression that ran along the crest of the hill in order to protect them against artillery. As the chaotic retreating Confederate forces reached Henry House Hill and General Bee saw Jackson's established brigade, he shouted, "There stands Jackson like a stone wall." Jackson suggested that Bee have his men fall in behind his own, and Bee rode through the disorderly mob urging them to rally behind 'Stonewall' Jackson. Not long after, a measure of order had been restored five intermingled Union brigades, nearly 10,000 strong, stormed the hill. The Confederates stood their ground. The Federals regrouped and charged again. The air was thick with gunsmoke as the battle raged at close range.

McDowell, erring badly, now ordered the Griffin and Ricketts artillery batteries up the hill. Exposed, and with the gunners under attack, Ricketts turned his guns upon the white frame house near the crest of the hill where he believed a sharpshooter was hiding. Spring Hill Farm belonged to the aged, bedridden Widow Henry (hence the name Henry House Hill). Judith Carter Henry became the first civilian casualty of the Civil War.

Meanwhile, Sherman began to feed his regiments into battle against Jackson. First the Wisconsin charged up the hill; as the regiment opened fire a blue-clad officer ran behind the gray-clad soldiers of Wisconsin telling them to hold their fire, that they were shooting their friends. Whether the officer was a blue-clad Confederate who thought they were Confederate soldiers shooting other Confederates, or a Union officer who thought the flag carried by the opposition was the Stars and Stripes, remains a mystery. But the effect was a momentary state of confusion that allowed Jackson to surge forward and caused the Wisconsin to retreat in even greater confusion.

Sherman next sent in the 79th New York. Up the hill they snaked through the dead and wounded. They were halfway up the hill when the first Confederate volley smashed into them. Colonel James Cameron, brother of the Secretary of War, shouted encouragement, and the men staggered on. Cameron fell with the next volley, which caused the men to

Union Colonel Michael Corcoran leads the "Gallant Sixty-ninth" in a costly assault on Confederate artillery at the First Battle of Bull Run. The battle proved to be a Union disaster.

fatter before they again pressed on. But then, as before, someone shouted that they were firing on their own men, that it was the Stars and Stripes that waved on the hill. An order was given to cease fire, and as 79th did, the Confederates hit them with everything they had, and Sherman's men went back down the hill at a run.

Demoralized by heavy losses to his brigade and disgusted by the fleeing amateur army, Sherman next sent up the 69th New York. They too were repelled. By this time the Union brigades were becoming badly jumbled, and to make matters worse, a trainload of Confederates reinforcements now arrived. These fresh troops, pitted against exhausted Federals who had either marched or fought since two in the morning, turned the tide. The Union forces started a general retreat toward Washington.

Things went from bad to worse. It was Sunday, and Washington had all but emptied as its citizens rode out to the easy slopes between Bull Run and Cub Run, about a mile east of the battlefield, to picnic and watch the Union soldiers whip the Rebels. They were not able to see much, and not until masses of dirt- and blood-caked soldiers, along with wagons and battery guns, appeared in a steady stream did it occur to the picnickers that it was time to get on the Turnpike and head for home. Then, when a lucky Rebel shell hit a wagon on the bridge over Cub Run and blocked it, panic ensued and the already disorderly retreat became a desperate rout.

Only two brigade commanders came away from Bull Run with their reputations enhanced: Stonewall Jackson and, though to a lesser extent, William Tecumseh Sherman. And Sherman, wounded in a knee and grazed on his shoulder, knew that neither side had much to be proud of. He knew, too, that the Union would never win this war with 90-day volunteer soldiers.

Above: *Federal encampment near Washington, DC, of the 7th New York Cavalry.*

Below: *Confederate General Stonewall Jackson at First Bull Run, where he acquired his nickname.*

Above: *The Old Stone House on a hill at Manassas, where the Confederates wavered briefly before turning the tide against the Federals.*

Left: *Union and Confederate soldiers battle fiercely on a wooden bridge prior to the Union retreat from Manassas to Washington, DC. At the First Battle of Bull Run, both armies were made up mainly of poorly trained volunteers.*

Bloody Shiloh

The defeat at Bull Run brought new leadership to the Union forces, for President Lincoln quickly replaced the luckless McDowell with Major General George McClellan. But as the East slipped back into a brief, uneasy calm, the focus of the war was shifting to the West, where the Union planned to take control of the Mississippi River, and to the troubled border states of Missouri and Kentucky that struggled to remain neutral. Both the Confederacy and the Union had raised troops within these two slave states, and each state had a home guard that would fight for whichever side with which the state finally aligned. Missouri had a pro-

Confederate governor but a pro-Union legislature; Kentucky's governor stood with the Union, while the majority of legislators supported the Confederate cause. Popular sentiment in both states was almost evenly divided, with some of the citizens siding with the Confederacy because of their common interest in maintaining slavery, while other slave-owners sided with the Union rather than risk seeing their land occupied by Federal troops and thus losing their slaves.

Up to this point the preservation of the country had been the only formal issue of the Civil War. If, however, the

Right: *General Irvin McDowell, first commander of the Union Army of the Potomac, lost his command after the defeat at the First Battle of Bull Run.*

to some of the boys. Blankets and tents were slow to arrive. Epidemics ran rampant through camp, for, unlike the big city Easterners Sherman had commanded near Washington, these farm boys from Indiana, Ohio and Illinois had lived in isolation most of their lives and were not immune from contagious diseases. Many of the soldiers, who were given scant rations and were expected to cook for themselves, were away from home for the first time and did not know the first thing about preparing food. If a company did not own an axe, which was true of many of them, firewood could not be chopped, hence the boys could not keep warm or stay dry.

Sherman worried incessantly about his troops' lack of discipline and lack of proper equipment and supplies. Most of all, now that he had, against his wishes, replaced Anderson, who had retired for health reasons, he was no longer just obeying orders – he was totally responsible. For hours he rode the land, mapping it, and he started doing other strange things. He exaggerated the enemy's strength and wired Lincoln repeatedly for more troops. Preoccupied and absent-minded, he smoked continually, sometimes two cigars at a time.

Above: *General George Brinton McClellan was given McDowell's former command. He was later to be general-in-chief.*

Right: *A well-equipped Union cavalryman. Equipment and supplies were always a major concern of Sherman.*

border states joined the Confederacy, the issue of slavery would be difficult to ignore. Both sides sent armies into the two border states hoping to win them over to their respective causes. In Kentucky the Confederates seized Columbus. Shortly afterward, Brigadier General Ulysses S. Grant marched down from Illinois and secured Paducah, Kentucky, for the Union. Lincoln then appointed Fort Sumter's former commandant, Brigadier General Robert Anderson, to Kentucky and the celebrated Western explorer Major General John C. Frémont to Missouri. Sherman had been promoted to brigadier general a few weeks after Bull Run, and Anderson now asked him to go with him to Kentucky as his right-hand man. Sherman agreed only after Lincoln promised that he would serve in a subordinate capacity and in no event was to be given a superior command.

Sherman hurried to Indiana and Illinois and begged the governors for recruits, but he soon learned that Frémont was already gathering them up as fast as they enlisted. He hurried to Frémont, a man he had detested since the old California days, but received no aid. Fortunately for Sherman, Frémont soon committed a grave mistake when he took it upon himself to proclaim freedom for the slaves of all owners who had rebelled against the Union. Lincoln, who was still trying to avoid making slavery an issue of the war, quickly annulled Fremont's proclamation and replaced him with Sherman's old friend Henry Halleck, who was more willing to share recruits.

Green troops brought Sherman a new set of troubles. The government, low on weapons, issued converted flintlocks

Cooking a meal at a winter encampment of the Union Army of the Potomac. The overwhelming resources of the North helped provide ample food and supplies to its troops in spite of the drain on civilian manpower.

Newspaper accounts of the Union's strength and his unfounded fear of the Confederate's strength convinced Sherman long before any one else that censorship was vital. The press, as now, enjoyed rights under the first amendment and did not take kindly to Sherman's new unilateral mandate imposing censorship on the press in his area of command. And because the gruff general had neither the patience nor time to coddle reporters, he soon made the press his life-long enemy.

The disgruntled press obtained a golden opportunity to crucify Sherman as the result of an incident that occurred when Secretary of War Simon Cameron stopped in Louisville. Sherman had taken Cameron and his entourage to his hotel rooms, dined them and, when Cameron asked to hear his troubles, Sherman asked to speak with him alone. Cameron insisted he talk in front of his friends. Reluctantly, Sherman locked the door and told the secretary that it would take 200,000 soldiers to secure the Mississippi valley. Misunderstanding, Cameron thought this number was in answer to his question about how many soldiers would it take to expel the enemy from Kentucky, and he was appalled. Although he promised to send troops and muskets right away, he later confided to a correspondent, who

was in the room when Sherman spoke, that he thought Sherman was crazy.

Newspapers gleefully latched on to Cameron's statement, and they were soon reporting on Sherman's unfortunate mental condition. He was replaced by Brigadier General Don Carlos Buell and ordered to St. Louis to join the Department of the Missouri, under Halleck's command. Ellen, who had been already become concerned from reading his agitated leters, traveled to St. Louis where she spoke to Halleck. Sherman was given leave to escort Ellen back to Ohio.

When a seemingly official report of Sherman's insanity appeared in the *Cincinnati Commercial* he felt disgraced. In Washington, both Tom Ewing and John Sherman demanded and received a retraction of the libelous article. When Sherman wrote to John about his thoughts of suicide, Tom Ewing gave him some fatherly advice. He told his outspoken son-on-law that he had overestimated the South's forces, that he should not dishearten Union men, that he should not voice kind feelings toward his Southern friends and that he sould stop saying things against Union policy. A calmer Sherman returned to duty with his foster father's words etched firmly on his mind.

Halleck welcomed Sherman to his Missouri command and made him his confidant. As they pored over maps at headquarters, Confederate General Albert Sidney Johnston was hastily building Fort Henry on the Tennessee River and Fort Donelson on the Cumberland River. Operating independently of Buell in Kentucky, Halleck sent Grant with

15,000 men in gunboats under Admiral Andrew H. Foote's command to take possession of Fort Henry, and its easy capture enhanced Union moral. Grant then marched overland toward Fort Donelson while Admiral Foote went upriver to destroy the Memphis and Ohio Railroad bridge.

Jubilantly Sherman sent men and supplies as well as encouragement to Grant, telling his junior in rank that if he could be of service at the front to send for him and he would waive his seniority. He was barely settled in his new headquarters at Paducah, Kentucky, when word arrived that Grant had captured Fort Donelson and taken at least 12,000 prisoners in the first conclusive Union victory of the war.

Grant had earned the nickname "Unconditional Surrender Grant" on February 16, 1862. Confederate General Simon Buckner, left in charge of Fort Donelson after Generals John Floyd and Gideon Pillow had fled with a brigade of 3000 men, had asked Grant the terms of surrender. Grant, who had been at West Point three years with Buckner and was afterward served with him in the army, replied, "Unconditional and immediate surrender."

The loss of Fort Donelson and the destruction of the railroad bridge across the Tennessee River cut off the Confederates from Tennessee and forced them back to Corinth, Mississippi. Lincoln was pleased, and on March 11, 1862, he promoted Halleck to be commander of all Union troops in the West. Halleck at once sent Sherman with Grant's troops southward up the Tennessee River to Pittsburg Landing. Soon afterward, he also sent Don Carlos Buell's troops to join the army, which was now encamped near Shiloh church. Halleck's plan was to take personal command of both armies and lead an offensive against the Confederates at Corinth, but Confederate General Albert Sidney Johnston had his own plans for an offensive against the Shiloh camp.

His April 6, 1861, surprise dawn attack brought mass confusion to the unsuspecting Union army. As Sherman, who held the de facto command at Camp Shiloh in Grant's tem-

Above: *General Ulysses S. Grant took Fort Donelson in the first decisive Union victory of the Civil War. Here he earned the nickname "Unconditional Surrender Grant" for the terms offered his old friend, the defeated Confederate General Simon Bolivar Buckner.*

Left: *General Grant watches as his army launches its assault on Fort Donelson.*

Opposite: *On the second day of the Battle of Shiloh, the 14th Regiment of Wisconsin Volunteers charges a New Orleans artillery battery. The battle took more lives than any other engagement in the war to that date.*

Right: *On the first day, the Hornet's Nest was the centre of Union resistance at Shiloh. Rebel forces attacked the position repeatedly before the Federals were forced to retreat.*

Below: *Maps showing troop movements on the first and second days at Shiloh.*

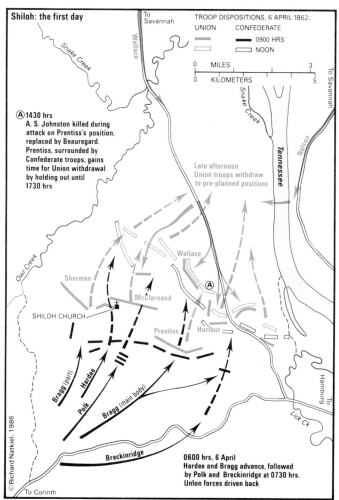

Shiloh: the first day

TROOP DISPOSITIONS, 6 APRIL 1862:
UNION   CONFEDERATE
0900 HRS
NOON

(A) 1430 hrs
A. S. Johnston killed during attack on Prentiss's position, replaced by Beauregard. Prentiss, surrounded by Confederate troops, gains time for Union withdrawal by holding out until 1730 hrs

Late afternoon Union troops withdraw to pre-planned positions

0600 hrs, 6 April
Hardee and Bragg advance, followed by Polk and Breckinridge at 0730 hrs. Union forces driven back

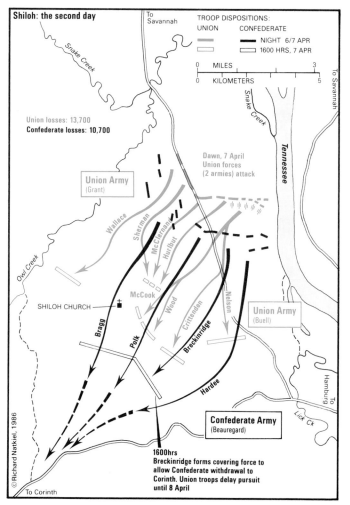

Shiloh: the second day

TROOP DISPOSITIONS:
UNION   CONFEDERATE
NIGHT 6/7 APR
1600 HRS, 7 APR

Union losses: 13,700
Confederate losses: 10,700

Union Army
(Grant)

Dawn, 7 April
Union forces
(2 armies) attack

Union Army
(Buell)

Confederate Army
(Beauregard)

1600hrs
Breckinridge forms covering force to allow Confederate withdrawal to Corinth. Union troops delay pursuit until 8 April

porary absence, looked through his field glasses and saw 40,000 Confederate troops three ranks deep advancing along a three-mile-wide front, he realized that he was in serious trouble. His efforts to rally his bewildered troops into some sort of coherent defensive line were in vain. They mainly ran from the enemy, and their being attacked by swarms of angry hornets from an area known as the Hornet's Nest did not help the situation. On hearing the shots Grant, who had gone into nearby Savannah to meet Buell, hurried back to find an estimated 8000 boys cowering under the bluffs by the river. He regrouped the soldiers and sent them back to the fighting.

Now that order had been restored, Sherman began to perform remarkably well. He held the line by reforming regiments as fast as they crumbled, drawing back step by step without letting the enemy break through. When hit in the hand, he merely wrapped a handkerchief around it. He had four horses shot from under him and narrowly escaped death when, as he leaned over to untangle the reins of his horse, a cannonball took off the brim at the back of his hat. When an aide of Grant arrived to ask how the battle was going, Sherman told him that if Grant had men to spare he could use them, otherwise he'd do the best he could. At ten in the morning, while Sherman was still receiving the brunt of the Confederacy's fury, Grant rode up to tell him that he had sent for more ammunition and was satisfied the line could be held. With that he rode off. In his memoirs Grant

wrote, "I never deemed it important to stay long with Sherman."

The bloody battle continued throughout the day. When surrounded, General Benjamin M. Prentiss, on Sherman's left, surrendered his remaining 2000 men, but the line still held, though it slowly yielded ground. At 2:30 the South received a blow when Confederate Commanding General Albert Sidney Johnston was killed in action, to be replaced by Beauregard. By nightfall the Federals were sitting on the river's edge barely holding on, while Confederates Bragg and Beauregard slept in Sherman's abandoned tent.

Yet this was to be the high point of Rebel fortunes at Shiloh. Beauregard found after the dawn roll call that he had left only half of his original 40,000 Confederates, whereas Grant had been reinforced by Generals Buell and Lew Wallace and now had an army of 55,000. The fight at bloody Shiloh continued throughout the drizzling second day, but now it was being fought increasingly on Union terms. At three in the afternoon Grant led one last charge, breaking the Confederates' resistance and sending them back to Corinth. It was a Union victory, but at an appalling cost. At Shiloh the losses were five times as heavy as at Bull Run – 13,000 Union and 10,700 Confederate casualties.

Sherman had won high praise and was promoted to major general. He had also won Grant's confidence. Thereafter, Grant and Sherman would become the North's answer to the South's Lee and Jackson.

Win the River, Win the War

With Shiloh behind him, with Halleck in Washington serving as General in Chief of the Union armies and with Grant commanding the Department of Tennessee, Sherman turned his attention to the Mississippi River. Like everyone else, he knew that controlling the river would cut the Confederacy in two. Divided, the South would eventually wither and die.

After Halleck's campaigns on the northern part of the Mississippi and Admiral Farragut's capture of New Orleans on April 25, 1862, the river was in fact now under Union control except for the vital 200 miles between Vicksburg and Port Hudson. But because those 200 miles remained under Confederate guns, merchant ships were cut off from the farmers in the Northwest, and the railroads were taking full advantage of their monopoly. Rash talk began to circulate of the Northwest seceding and forming its own federation in order to make peace with the Confederate States and regain access to the cheaper water freight.

Both Grant and Sherman realized that the capture of Vicksburg was the key to the situation, but, before he had left, Halleck had spread the army over such a wide area that only 35,000 men could be gathered for a campaign against the city. Both generals knew that they would have to wait for more troops, and even then, taking Vicksburg would not be easy, for nature as well as the Confederates had fortified her. Vicksburg's high bluffs overlooking a giant hairpin curve in the river made an ideal location for Confederate batteries, which in turn made a naval assault hazardous. The lowlands to the southwest and northeast consisted of swamps and bayous, making a land assault difficult.

Never one to give up, Sherman sent a plan to Grant. He would march south along the railroad tracks, 40 miles to the east, that ran between Memphis and Vicksburg, while another force floated down the Mississippi. Vicksburg would be surrounded. Grant liked the plan and, if he had his way, would soon have the forces to implement it.

The forces he had in mind were being recruited in the troubled Northwest by Major General John McClernand. McClernand, an ambitious former congressman from Illinois, had asked Lincoln in September, 1862, for a commission to raise an army for the purpose of capturing Vicksburg, thereby opening the Mississippi and saving the Northwest from secession. Lincoln, unwilling to alienate such a powerful political force in the Northwest, had agreed. McClernand, who had served well beside Sherman at Shiloh, then swept through the Northwest rekindling the recruiting fires that hitherto had been all but extinguished. Soon he had 60,000 under his command.

Grant telegraphed Halleck of his plans to take Vicksburg and asked for reinforcements. Halleck was silent. Grant

Far left: *General Halleck was appointed Union general-in-chief in 1862.*

Left: *Lincoln, with McClernand and Allen Pinkerton.*

Above: *Union army engineers build a pontoon bridge across a river. A shortage of bridge sections slowed Sherman's movements in the assault on Vicksburg.*

telegraphed again that he would attack without reinforcements if they didn't come at once. Halleck wired that twelve regiments would soon be in Memphis. Grant further queried Halleck as to whether he should command the expedition down the river himself or send Sherman. He was told to do as he thought best. Grant would send Sherman: he knew McClernand was Sherman's senior but doubted the former's fitness for command, since McClernand was not a West Pointer and had received his generalship through political favors.

On December 18 Grant received orders from Halleck to divide his command into four corps, with McClernand to command the amphibious operation. Although this interfered with his plans, Grant obeyed orders and sent McClernand a telegram informing him of his new command. But the communication did not get through to him because Confederate cavalry had fortuitously cut the wires, and, although Halleck had sent orders to Grant on the 18th, he did not get around to sending a copy of them to McClernand (in Springfield, Illinois) until the 22nd. When McClernand finally received word he started south the next day with his new bride and the bridal party. On the 26th he docked at Memphis, only to find his men gone. Sherman had sailed off with them on the 19th.

A disgruntled McClernand was the least of Grant's and Sherman's troubles. Grant's march overland toward Vicksburg with 40,000 men was constantly harassed by Confederate General John Pemberton's 22,000-man Army of Mississippi. One of Pemberton's subordinates, General Earl Van Dorn, with 3500 cavalrymen swept behind Grant and captured his supply depot at Holly Springs. At the same time, cavalryman General Nathan Bedford Forrest, a one-time slave dealer, ripped up track, cut telegraph lines and seized Union weapons and equipment. Cut off, Grant was unable to get word to Sherman that his part of the campaign was a failure.

If Grant's part of the campaign could be termed a failure, Sherman's first independent campaign was even worse. In his hurry to steal away Sherman had forgotten sections of pontoon bridges, and this oversight reduced his options and slowed his progress. In heavy rains, he landed his 32,000 men just north of Vicksburg on a swampy, heavily wooded area encircled by bayous. On the 29th he charged Chickasaw Bluffs. The attack was quickly repulsed, costing him over 1700 men to the Confederates' 200. He had not known that Pemberton had transported his men to Vicksburg to deal with Sherman after disposing of Grant. So now, with the help of Admiral Porter's gunboats, Sherman strengthened his position below the bluffs and waited for the sounds of battle from Grant in the east.

Sherman's wait would have been long had McClernand not finally caught up with him. McClernand at once assumed command and divided the army into two corps, one under Sherman, the other under General George Morgan. Then, for lack of anything better and wanting a quick victory, McClernand took Sherman's suggestion and stormed Fort Hindman on the Arkansas River. The oper-

Above: *Admiral Porter's Union flotilla of 18 gunboats runs the Confederate batteries at Vicksburg.*

Right: *Admiral David Dixon Porter supported the Union assault on Vicksburg. Of his 18 vessels, 11 survived the Confederate shore batteries.*

ation was a success; not only did McClernand capture the fort, he captured 5000 Confederates as well. McClernand was very pleased with himself, but Sherman and Porter were not. They begged Grant to come to Vicksburg and take command.

Grant arrived late in January, 1863, to find McClernand camped at Milliken's Bend and Young's Point, about 12 miles above Vicksburg on the Mississippi. Grant's choices were now limited. He would have liked to try another overland campaign to the east of Vicksburg, but in order to get the men in position to start again he would have to boat them upriver to Memphis, which would look like a retreat (another defeat on the heels of Fredericksburg and Murfreesboro would just about ruin Lincoln) and give the anti-Sherman Northern newspapers more fuel. (Sherman had just arrested a correspondent and ordered him court-martialed as a spy.) It looked as if he would have to launch an assault from the river, and from the wrong side of the river at that. Knowing that if he failed, his army, if not the war, would most likely be lost, Grant continued to look for alternatives to a direct assault against the heavily fortified bluffs to the north of Vicksburg.

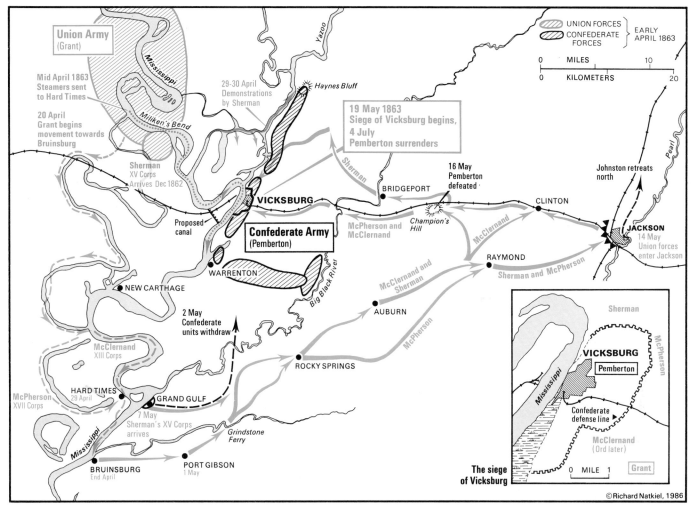

Map of the Siege of Vicksburg, showing the Confederate positions and Union movements, including Sherman's rush to aid McPherson at Jackson and his march west to beat the retreating Rebels to the bluffs north of the city.

He divided 60,000 men into three corps under the leadership of McClernand, Sherman and James B. McPherson. While the others explored the bayous and tributaries for a back door route into Vicksburg, Sherman resumed work on a canal that had been begun the summer before. The object of the canal across the DeSoto peninsula, opposite Vicksburg on the west shore of the Mississippi, was to redirect the river's flow and bypass Vicksburg. Sherman detailed 500 men a day to work on the canal. The threat of drowning in the ever-rising water, disease and abominable living conditions were no help to morale, and after two months of hard work it became obvious that the Mississippi could not be turned. The project was abandoned in March, 1863.

Fifty miles upriver from Vicksburg another canal was cut across to Lake Providence in hope that if the Mississippi were connected with the lake it would then follow a series of bayous and rivers to the Red River, making possible an amphibious attack on Vicksburg from the south. When receding waters threatened, and shallow-bottom boats could not be obtained to accommodate so many men, this project was also abandoned.

Still Grant continued to hunt for his back door. Three hundred miles north of Vicksburg a levee was cut, allowing gunboats and transports to get into the Yazoo River, float down to a landing point away from the fortified bluffs, and take Vicksburg. Unfortunately, the boats could not get beyond Fort Pemberton. Near the mouth of the Yazoo was a network of tributaries, and Sherman and Porter next tried cruising down a combination of these. But the gunboats became tangled with trees in narrow channels, and Rebels felled trees behind them to cut off their escape route. They succeeded in backing out, but narrowly avoided disaster.

Desperate, Grant turned to his last remaining plan. Leaving Sherman's corps at the bluffs as a decoy, and having Grierson's cavalry ride from Grand Junction, Tennessee, through the eastern part of Mississippi down to Baton Rouge, Louisiana, to distract Confederate attention, Grant marched the other two corps downriver, on the Louisiana side, through the swamps and bayous, building roads and bridges engineers would have been proud to claim. Meanwhile, on the dark night of April 16, 1863, Admiral Porter ran his entire fleet past a firestorm from the Vicksburg batteries. Amazingly, he suffered the loss of only one ship. Downriver at Hard Times Landing, Porter picked up Grant and 33,000 of his troops and transported them ten miles south and then across the river to Bruinsburg. Having learned a lesson on his winter overland march, Grant abandoned his supply base and foraged on his march northeast toward Jackson, Mississippi, where he hoped to destroy Vicksburg's source of supplies before he turned due west to begin the siege of Vicksburg itself.

Meanwhile, Sherman gathered his forces and put them on the decks of the transports, telling them to look and sound as numerous as possible, and steamed past a Confederate

Left: *An elaborate system of Union trenches surrounded Vicksburg by the beginning of June. Grant's siege ended in the surrender of the weary Confederates on July 4, 1863.*

Above: *Union soldiers charge into a breach created by an explosion on Fort Hill, one of Vicksburg's defences. Fortifications around the city formed a line about nine miles long.*

garrison atop Haynes' Bluff. Sherman then landed the men, marched them back up the river through the woods, put them on transports and again floated them past the garrison. As a result, Confederate General Pemberton was told that Grant's march was just a ruse and that the real danger lay to the north of Vicksburg. The large detachment that had been sent to repulse Grant was therefore recalled and returned just in time to watch Sherman march his men south toward the boats and sail away to join Grant.

Timing was on the Union's side. Confederate General Joe Johnston had been sent west to take general command of Pemberton's and Bragg's armies, but he was not certain what Grant was up to, and when he finally realized that Pemberton would now almost certainly lose his army as well as Vicksburg, he sent word to Pemberton to leave the city and join him. But Confederate President Jefferson Davis had ordered Pemberton to hold Vicksburg at all costs. So instead of heading north to join Johnston, Pemberton headed east to confront Grant.

Sherman had marched at the double-quick in order to join Grant before Johnston could reach Pemberton. Sherman then continued at an incredible speed to aid McPherson against Johnston's weaker defensive army at Jackson. After burning everything they could not use, Sherman and McPherson turned west and began yet another amazing high-speed march towards Vicksburg.

As Sherman was hurrying towards Vicksburg, Grant joined battle with Pemberton on May 16 at Champion's Hill. Grar.t had the advantage of knowing Pemberton's plans, having been sold a copy of Johnston's orders by a Confederate courier, yet McClernand's Federal corps had to struggle until McPherson's corps stormed the Confeder-

ate's flank and pushed Pemberton back. His retreat turned into a rout equal to that at Bull Run. An entire division became so totally cut off from the rest of the Confederate army that it had to break away and flee north to join Johnston.

Sherman's corps, meantime, had managed to beat the retreating Confederates to the bluffs north of Vicksburg, which Pemberton had evacuated because he needed most of the men to battle Grant. Now the Federals finally had a docking place on the same side of the river as their objective, and Grant could be easily reinforced and resupplied.

On May 19, 1863, Grant ordered the first assault on of the Confederate trenches. Sherman was repulsed, losing over 1000 men. Three days later all three corps charged. Again they failed. (McClernand had so bungled this second attack that Grant replaced him with General Edward Ord.) Discouraged, Grant ordered trenches dug; he would simply sit out the siege.

Vicksburg was entirely cut off. Pemberton was helpless; the best he could hope for was to hold out until Johnston came to the rescue. Johnston *was* building up his army, but so was Grant, and Johnston soon realized that not only was

Vicksburg lost, so was Pemberton's army.

For 44 days both the troops and the citizens in Vicksburg endured starvation, thirst, constant shellfire from Porter's fleet and extreme mental distress. Some of the citizens moved into caves in the sides of cliffs for protection against the mortars. On July 3, 1863, Pemberton asked Grant the terms of surrender. Grant gave him his pat answer, "Unconditional and Immediate surrender." Pemberton was not ready for such terms. He was, however, ready to surrender everything if his soldiers were released on parole. Grant considered. Sending 30,000 men to prison camps in the north would tie up his boats, and the starved soldiers were probably no longer fit for duty anyway, and would, no doubt, return to their homes. (Grant's logic was sound, but there are accounts of Southern soldiers surrendering in as many as five battles.) So Grant agreed, and on the following day, Independence Day, at the same moment that Lee was retreating from Gettysburg, Grant at long last marched his troops into Vicksburg. Four days later Port Hudson, the final stronghold on the Mississippi, fell. The Confederacy was now vertically split in two.

Above: *A panoramic view of the Union siege of Vicksburg. When it fell, the South lost the key city guarding the Mississippi between Memphis and New Orleans.*

Right: *Union attack on Port Hudson, Louisiana, the last Confederate bastion on the Mississippi. It surrendered four days after Vicksburg, and the Confederacy was now split in two.*

The Horizontal Division

In September, 1863, Sherman again found himself in a position he did not relish. With Grant incapacitated by a fall from a horse in New Orleans, Sherman was left holding the reins of command. And nothing was going his way. Most of all, Sherman was angry at Halleck for not allowing him to go on the offensive. Union forces had been successful at dividing the south vertically along the Mississippi, and now Sherman felt they should divide it again horizontally, in order to weaken it further. Instead, Halleck, who had always been slow to initiate battle, scattered Grant's army as garrisons in the conquered areas. Only personal loyalty to his old friend kept Sherman from speaking out against Halleck's military policies.

Still angry, Sherman sat down and wrote a 2700-word essay at Halleck's request giving his views on how best to deal with the occupied states. Lincoln was so taken with it

that he requested Halleck to ask Sherman if he could publish it. Surprising no one, Sherman replied that he did not like to see his name in print.

Then news came of the Union defeat at Chickamauga Creek. General William Rosecrans' Army of the Cumberland had taken Chattanooga from the fleeing Confederate General Braxton Bragg, but then the 60,000 Federals had spread over a 40-mile front in pursuit of Bragg. Bragg, however, had been reinforced to the tune of 60,000 men by Simon Buckner from east Tennessee, detachments from Johnston and divisions from Lee's Army of Northern Virginia. On September 19-20, 1863, a battle had been fought at Chickamauga Creek. Of the Federals, only George Thomas's corps had stood tall, earning him the nickname "Rock of Chickamauga". Casualties were high: 18,000 Confederates and 16,000 Federals. Rosecrans had retreated to Chatta-

Above: *For his service at Vicksburg, Sherman was made a brigadier general, and when Grant was placed in command of the West, Sherman became commander of the Army of the Tennessee. Soon he was sent to assist Grant in the rescue of the Union forces under siege at Chattanooga.*

Right: *Union General William S. Rosecrans had captured Chattanooga from retreating Rebels but later was himself besieged there. He is shown here as the victor in the earlier battle of Stone's River, Tennessee.*

nooga, where he was now under siege, and Sherman, with 20,000 troops, was ordered to help him.

While Sherman, at his camp on the Big Black River near Vicksburg, was preparing for the march, personal tragedy found him. Sherman's wife and children were visiting. Together the family took the last transport from Vicksburg to Memphis, whence he would go on to Chattanooga and they to Lancaster. Nine-year-old Willie, Sherman's most precious, fell ill during the boat ride and died 24 hours after reaching Memphis. Because of the preparations for his

Above: *View of Chattanooga, with Lookout Mountain in the background. Important to the Confederacy as a major railroad junction, its loss would split the southeast and give Union forces access to Georgia and Alabama.*

Overleaf: *General Sherman's headquarters in Chattanooga.*

Right: *The men of the Union Army of the Cumberland swarm up the slopes of Missionary Ridge on November 25, 1863, overrunning line after line of Rebel defenses.*

Below: *A part of the battlefield at Missionary Ridge.*

march to Chattanooga, Sherman hardly had time to give way to his grief. He obtained a metal casket, attended a military funeral – with the Thirteenth Cavalry escorting their mascot's body to the steamboat – and saw Minnie, Lizzie, Tom, Mrs. Sherman and Willie's casket off. Willie was buried in Lancaster, but in 1867 his body was moved to the Calvary Cemetery in St. Louis, where the Thirteenth erected a marble monument over their honorary sergeant's grave. Sherman would remember the Thirteenth's kindness the rest of life.

Putting his personal suffering aside, Sherman started toward Chattanooga. If nothing else, Sherman could take comfort in knowing that he was now on the offensive and that the defeat at Chickamauga had forced Lincoln and Halleck to make two important decisions. They had sent General Joe Hooker to Chattanooga with a corps from the Army of the Potomac and had promoted Grant to overall command in the West. From his New Orleans sickbed Grant wired Chattanooga, replacing Rosecrans with Thomas. His second wire informed Sherman that the command of the Department and Army of the Tennessee, of which Sherman had so reluctantly assumed temporary command, was now formally his.

Sherman's progress to Chattanooga was slow, but at last he joined Grant there on November 15. Grant had arrived in Chattanooga on October 23 to find Thomas's men on quarter-rations. He had made a supply route his first priority. Before dawn on October 27 Union Brigadier General W. F. Smith with 3500 men had drifted on pontoon rafts past sentries and charged ashore at Brown's Ferry. Building a pontoon bridge, the Federals had then established a line of supply labeled "the cracker line."

The capture of Lookout Mountain, only lightly defended by the Confederates, gave the Union army control of important high ground and set the stage for the attack on Missionary Ridge on the following day.

With Sherman's arrival and that of General Joseph Hooker's corps before him, Grant now had 70,000 men to Bragg's 40,000. His plan was to have Hooker keep the Confederates busy at Lookout Mountain on the left, and Thomas to do the same at Orchard Knob in front of Missionary Ridge, while Sherman attacked the right flank at Tunnel Hill. On November 23 Thomas took Orchard Knob. The next day Hooker fought in a heavy fog on the slopes of Lookout Mountain. After dark the outnumbered rebels fell back to Missionary Ridge. At down on the 25th Sherman attacked Tunnel Hill. Unfortunately, his opponent, Major General Patrick Cleburne, was one of the best the Confederates had. For more than eight hours Sherman battled him. Even when Oliver Howard's two divisions came to Sherman's aid, no gain was made. Fearing Cleburne might counterattack if reinforced from the middle, Grant ordered Thomas to move against the rifle pits at the base of Missionary Ridge as a diversion. The besieged men of the Army of the Cumberland had been chomping at the bit; now they had their chance. Even the non-combat personnel found arms and went into battle. After taking the pits, without orders they charged the steep ridge itself, shouting "Chickamauga." Over Bragg's protests the Confederates rereated in confusion as the angry Federals scrambled over the crest. Bragg, who barely escaped capture, would not escape Jefferson Davis' wrath.

Phil Sheridan's cavalry, along with Sherman and Hooker, pursued the routed rebels, capturing between 4000 and 6000 prisoners, numerous weapons and supply wagons. Grant had just started counting the spoils when the message from Lincoln arrived congratulating him and ordering him to send assistance to Ambrose Burnside, who was now under siege in Knoxville. Grant at first thought of sending General Gordon Granger's corps toward Knoxville, but he shortly after decided that only Sherman could get to Knoxville in time to save Burnside, who had only three days' food supply.

Sherman pressed his exhausted troops – some without shoes – through the rocky country over muddy and icy roads. His freezing men, who ate only what they could gather along the road, had to cover 85 miles in three days. On the third day, 40 miles short, he sent his cavalry ahead, telling them to "push into Knoxville at whatever cost of life and horse-flesh." To their surprise they found Burnside doing just fine. Indeed, his men were much better fed and clothed than Sherman's, for they had just won a battle with the enemy and had sent them off to the hills to lick their wounds.

Sherman then sent his troops to winter quarters along the Tennessee River, while he went home to mourn with his family over Willie's death. At home he found himself mobbed by well-wishers, autograph-seekers, reporters, photographers and hand-shakers. Catching up on newspaper reading, Sherman discovered that a long letter he had written to Lincoln had been in vain. The President had done just the opposite of what Sherman had advised: Lincoln had decided not to wait until after the war to return occupied territory to its citizens. The biggest thing he learned, however, was that Grant was now more powerful in military matters than either Halleck or Lincoln. Sherman had always felt the Union had not recognized the vital importance of Grant's victory at Vicksburg, the more spectacular stand at Gettysburg no doubt having overshadowed the victory. Ironically, the taking of Chattanooga's Missionary Ridge on mob impulse had made of Grant the national hero he should have been after Vicksburg. Sherman wrote Grant that it was imperative for him to stay alive, for when the war came to a close he alone would have the power to "heal and mend up the breaches made by war."

Back from leave, Sherman set out for Meridian, Mississippi, a hotbed of guerrilla activities 150 miles east of Vicksburg. On February 14, 1864, he marched into Meridian with little resistance. There he found huge quantities of food, arms and clothing, which he either destroyed or carried off. Confederates later charged that he had confiscated 300 wagons to carry the supplies he stole and that he had carried off 8000 slaves, many of them on stolen horses and mules. Sherman claimed only the 500 prisoners he brought back; he referred to those following his column as ten miles of Negroes. He did, however, acknowledged destroying 25 miles of railroad in all directions, something the Confederates neglected to advertise.

Above: *Ruins of a Nashville and Chattanooga Railroad bridge. Both sides in the war attempted to disrupt enemy transportation.*

Left: *Union Generals Sherman, Sheridan and Grant.*

Overleaf: *General Ulysses S. Grant (lower left) with his staff on Lookout Mountain.*

Total War

The spring of 1864 found changes on both sides. Lincoln issued a draft call for 500,000 more soldiers. Grant replaced Halleck as commander of all Union armies, Sherman replaced Grant as commanding general of the Military Division of the Mississippi and Confederate General Joseph E. Johnston replaced Braxton Bragg as the commander of the Confederate Army of Tennessee. More important, a new type of warfare was being planned – total war. Sherman, remembering his days in Florida as a young lieutenant in the Seminole Wars, recognized that for the Union to win, the will of the South had to be broken. And the way to break the South's will was to strip it of everything needed to engage in war. Almost everything would henceforth be treated as a military target: transportation networks, industrial plants, cotton exports, food, even shelter. He felt certain that by having the full wright of war fall on the civilians, the spirit of the Confederacy would crumble faster than any other way.

To help Sherman carry out his plan were the 60,000-man Army of the Cumberland under Major General George Thomas, the Army of the Tennessee led by Major General James McPherson with 30,000 and the Army of the Ohio commanded by Major General John Schofield and numbering 17,000.

Knowing this force was not large enough to be everywhere at once, Sherman decided the next best thing would be to show the Confederates that it could go anywhere he chose. He was confident that his force could accomplish the feat: hadn't Grant cut his own supply line and lived off the land during the Vicksburg campaign?

Also important was the need for another decisive victory.

Right: *Union General George H. Thomas, commanding the Army of the Cumberland, served under Sherman in the Atlanta Campaign.*

ing Sherman's march to Atlanta were General Johnston's three corps, commanded by Generals William Hardee, John Hood and Leonidas Polk. Sherman, logistically supported by the railroad line, maneuvered skillfully, skirting Johnston's forces whenever possible. Johnston's goal was to keep him out of Atlanta, at least until after the election. Although they skirmished constantly, Sherman would be able to involve Johnston in only three significant battles: Resaca, on May 13-15, New Hope Church, on May 25-28, and Kennesaw Mountain, on June 27.

Johnston's primary problem was dealing with Sherman, but President Davis was a secondary one. Johnston, who had had some success revitalizing Bragg's army, was not a favorite of Davis, and the Confederate president continually harassed Johnston, demanding that he take the offensive. In the end, this interference would contribute heavily to the fall of Atlanta. To mollify the president, Johnston sent General Nathan Forrest – considered the greatest American cavalryman even though lacking any formal education – to conduct raids in Mississippi and Tennessee. These raids turned out to be brilliant operations, irritating Sherman considerably. On the other hand, too add to Johnston's problems, a member of his staff, General John B. Hood, was writing secret dispatches to Jefferson Davis.

Above: *Confederate President Jefferson Davis interfered in Johnston's battle plans, demanding that he take the offensive.*

Right: *Confederate General Joseph E. Johnston opposed Sherman with three corps, under Hood, Polk and Hardee.*

With former General McClellan – who promised some kind of accommodation with the South that would suit the war-weary voters – challenging Lincoln in the upcoming election, Lincoln's best political hope lay in a military triumph.

With this in mind, Grant planned two campaigns for 1864. With the Army of the Potomac under General George Meade as acting commander and with General Sheridan as commander of the cavalry, he would confront Lee's Army of Northern Virginia and try to capture Richmond. Sherman, meanwhile, was to march through the agricultural and industrial heartland of the South, splitting it yet again and crushing Atlanta, the supply, manufacturing and communications center.

Opposing Grant and Sherman would be the two strongest armies in the South, those of General Robert E. Lee and General Joseph E. Johnston. Henceforth the fate of the nation would depend on the successes of these four men. The two Southern generals, with roughly 65,000 soldiers each, would be cast as defensive players in the new game of total war; Grant and Sherman, commanding 100,000 men each, would play the offense.

On May 4, 1864, the day that Grant launched his campaign against Lee, Sherman advanced from Chattanooga. Oppos-

Above: *Confederate General John Bell Hood commanded a corps under Johnston and succeeded him as commander in defense of Atlanta.*

Above right: *Union General James B. McPherson commanded the Army of the Tennessee under Sherman. He had been a classmate of Hood.*

Johnston was not the only one with problems. Sherman was also faced with in-house troubles. Hooker, who had come from the East with the Army of the Potomac to help at Chattanooga, seemed jealous – according to Sherman in his memoirs – of the West's commanders. He wrote Sherman on June 22 that he had repulsed two heavy attacks, was apprehensive about his extreme right flank and that three entire corps were in front of him. In the first place, Sherman was unhappy to receive a note that should have been sent to Thomas, to whom Hooker's corps belonged. Second, he knew that Schofield was supposed to be protecting Hooker's right flank. Third, Sherman knew it impossible for three corps to be in front of Hooker. Sherman, with Schofield and Hooker, hashed it out. Schofield angrily protested that his own men were actually in advance of Hooker's line and offered to show Sherman that his dead men were lying farther out than any of Hooker's. Wrote Sherman, "General Hooker pretended not to have known this fact . . . I told him that such a thing must not occur again . . . I reproved him reproved him more gently than the occasion demanded, and from that time he began to sulk."

To add to everything else, Sherman received word that his seventh child, Charles, had been born but was frail and was not expected to survive. During his march to the sea in December he would read of the death of the son he had never seen in a Southern newspaper. The child's body, originally buried at Notre Dame, in South Bend, Indiana, would in 1867 be moved to St Louis to rest along with Sherman's beloved Willie. Sherman could not, however, take time to grieve for the child he had hoped would fill the void left by Willie's death; he held the lives of other men's children in his hands. Johnston's strategy had to be Sherman's sole concern.

Johnston's first position was atop Rocky Face Ridge in front of Dalton, Georgia. Sherman looked up at the cannon and down the narrow pass, known as Buzzard Roost, and weighed his options. His plan was to use Thomas' army as decoy in front of Johnston, while McPherson, flanking wide, marched his men through Snake Creek Gap to Resaca in order to seize the town and railroad line and block Johnston's line of retreat toward Atlanta. Thomas kept up his end of the plan, but McPherson, overestimating the garrison's strength, retreated to Snake Creek Gap when confronted with a mere 4000 Confederate defenders.

When word reached Johnston that a Federal army was at his rear, he quickly fell back to Resaca. Sherman moved Thomas and Schofield in for the May 13-15 attack. Thereafter, seeing no advantage in continuing the fruitless battle, Sherman flanked the town and continued his relentless march to Atlanta. Johnston pulled up stakes and raced south through the wooded and rugged country to find another place to repulse the advancing Federals.

Finding such a spot where two roads met between Kingston and Cassville, Johnston deployed his men and waited to spring the trap. But Sherman spread out his troops like a fan and did not come down the road in a column. Hood and Polk, claiming they were now flanked, persuaded Johnston to fall back to Allatoona. As Sherman brushed brushed past his left, Johnston sent his cavalry to raid Sherman's supply line, but Sherman's three armies eventually converged at Dallas and fought a series of successful battles at New Hope Church, Pumpkin Vine Creek and Pickett's Mills. Sherman, who had explored Georgia as a young lieutenant, had slipped nimbly through Johnston's grasp and had reached the railroad line.

From this point on he was able to repair track as fast as Johnston could destroy it. He was so successful, indeed, that Southern folklore has it that Sherman's men carried extra bridges and tunnels with them. But still threatening Sherman's supply line was Forrest, back in Tennessee and Mississippi, and so great an irritant was he that Sherman wrote to Stanton that Forrest should be followed to the death, even if it cost 10,000 lives and broke the Treasury.

As incessant rains slowed both armies, Johnston pulled

back to Kennesaw Mountain, near Marietta, and prepared for Sherman's arrival. Here, during a Confederate staff conference on June 14, Leonidas Polk was killed by Federal artillery. After the war Johnston recounted the incident to Sherman, saying that he had noticed Sherman's battery was about to fire and had cautioned his officers to scatter. They did so, but the dignified Polk, not wishing to appear hurried or fearful in front of his men, had walked away slowly and was struck in the chest by an unexploded shell that killed him instantly.

Because of rain it took Sherman until June 27 to prepare for the Kennesaw battle. It could have been avoided if he had flanked Johnston as he had done so often previously, but now Sherman elected a frontal assault. His decision was based on a number of reasons: the roads were muddy and the river banks overflowed, making a fast march impossible; the Federals had been marching seven weeks under constant harassment and were tired; and the troops knew they outnumbered the Confederates and wanted a victory.

Featuring it would not be prudent to stretch out too far, Sherman had his three armies attack in columns, and by nine in the morning the troops were moving along a ten-mile line. McPherson's army fought up the face of the lesser Kennesaw on the Confederate right but could not reach the summit. A mile away, Thomas sent his army in two columns against the Confederate center. Schofield moved slowly on the Confederate left. By 11:30 that morning the battle was over, and the result was a disastrous 2500 Federal loss to the Confederate's 800.

Scarcely stopping to regroup, Sherman sent McPherson east around the Confederate's right flank over drying roads toward Roswell and the Chattahoochee River. Johnston detected the movement and abandoned Kennesaw. According to Sherman's memoirs, he quickly pursued, "hoping to catch Johnston in the confusion of retreat, especially at the crossing of the Chattahoochee River." But Johnston's position on the river looked strong, and, rather than confronting it directly, Sherman's troops made a feint to the right, then advanced and crossed the river on the left flank. Unable to counter, Johnston withdrew to the elaborate earthworks fortifying Atlanta. Here he hoped to hold out until the Union elections. Sherman hoped otherwise.

Below: *Sherman's advance on Atlanta was delayed by his preparations for the battle at Kennesaw Mountain, where the Rebel army was entrenched.*

Overleaf: *The battleground at New Hope Church. Here Johnston held Sherman off valiantly but finally had to retreat to Kennesaw Mountain.*

The Fall of Atlanta

On July 17, 1864, President Davis ordered Johnston to turn over the command of the Army of Tennessee to John Bell Hood. Sherman could not have been more delighted had he made the appointment himself. Sherman was confident that the impetuous Hood would go over to the offensive and hence fight outside of the nearly impregnable fortifications around the city. Both McPherson and Schofield had been classmates of Hood at West Point, and Sherman and his two generals discussed Hood at great length. Of Hood, Sherman wrote: "We agreed that we ought to be unusually cautious and prepared at all times for sallies and for hard fighting, because Hood, though not deemed much of a scholar, or of great mental capacity, was undoubtedly a brave, determined, and rash man."

Not wanting Hood to be reinforced by troops from Lee's army, Sherman sent Schofield and McPherson eastward toward Decatur to break up the Georgia railroad lines, while Thomas moved slowly across Peachtree Creek toward Atlanta. The result was that a gap of several miles developed, a serious mistake which Hood quickly spotted. He immediately moved in and struck Thomas, hitting him hard for four hours at close range. Thomas, who had fortunately crossed Peachtree Creek and was in a good defensive position before Hardee's and A. P. Stewart's corps attacked him, brought up his guns and repelled the Confederates. Each side had roughly 20,000 men; Federal losses were about 1800 to the Confederates' 4800.

While his troops were fighting the Confederates, Sherman was protesting Washington's policy of enlisting Negro soldiers. Sherman, who was hiring fugitive slaves at $10 a month to do heavy labor, ordered a recruiting agent arrested for offering $14 a month to black enlistees. Secretary of War Edwin Stanton heard about it and was angry, but in his own defense Sherman insisted that it was wrong to take Negro men away from their women, leaving "black paupers on our hands." When Negroes wanted to know where to join up, Sherman referred them to eight cities – all

deep in Confederate-controlled territory. Lincoln wrote and asked Sherman to reconsider but fared no better. Someone suggested that a Negro was as good as a white man at stopping a bullet. Sherman countered that a sandbag was preferable. So Sherman again found himself in the newspapers again, this time attacked by outraged Abolitionists and even praised by some Confederates.

Having fallen back to the fortifications around Atlanta, Hood learned of McPherson's exposed position east of town and seized his second chance to mount an attack on July 22. He sent Hardee's weary troops south out of Atlanta on a 15-mile march to fall on McPherson's flank. But Hardee did not catch McPherson's army on the left flank because two divisions of Grenville Dodge's corps had been sent during the night to extend it. McPherson was with Sherman when the firing began. He hastily gathered his papers into a small book, pocketed it and jumped on his horse, telling Sherman he would send back word. Sherman paced up and down the porch of his headquarters, waiting for news. Soon a staff officer reported that McPherson's horse had returned bleeding and riderless.

Years later Sherman received a letter from an eye-witness to McPherson's death. The general had dressed his lines and then had ridden into a group of Confederate skirmishers. They called for the Yankees to halt; McPherson raised his hat in salute and then quickly bolted. He was immediately shot from his horse. Sherman wept when an hour later the body was brought to him and placed on a door wrenched from its hinges. As a doctor and Sherman examined the wound under his heart, Sherman realized in dismay that the book containing his papers was missing. Fortunately, it was found the next day in the haversack of a Confederate prisoner.

Meanwhile, the battle raged on into the evening, with the Federals repelling both frontal and rear attacks by the determined Confederates. Finally, realizing his flank attack was a failure, Hood broke off the fighting with the loss of

Above: *Confederate troops under S D Lee set upon Howard's Union forces at Ezra Church on July 28, 1864. The attack was repulsed, but it prevented Howard from cutting the rail line.*

Right: *Part of Confederate lines defending Atlanta against Sherman.*

Below: *View of the city of Atlanta as it appeared on the eve of the evacuation of its civilian population.*

Above: *At Jonesboro, Georgia, 15 miles south of Atlanta, a Union attack on August 31 resulted in 3000 Confederate dead and 2000 captured.*

Right: *Rebel troops captured at Jonesboro being marched to Atlanta.*

8000 of the 37,000 engaged. The Federal's 30,000 had suffered 3722 casualties and had held their ground against superior numbers.

Kennesaw Mountain had taught Sherman that frontal assaults against strong fortifications were useless. Instead of another attack, he attempted to tighten the siege around Atlanta by cutting the railroads to the south, sending 10,000 cavalry under Edward McCook and George Stoneman for that purpose. Stoneman begged Sherman to allow him to ride on to Andersonville after cutting the lines in order to

rescue the 30,000 Federal prisoners held three, and Sherman, for once following his heart instead of his head, consented. Apparently neither of them stopped to think of so many weakened men trying to walk 130 miles through hostile territory. Not that it mattered; McCook's division was routed and dispersed, and Stoneman, with 700 reserves, covered the escape of two small brigades before surrendering and becoming a prisoner himself.

Sherman now tried another tactic. He ordered Oliver Howard, McPherson's replacement, to march north, completely around the city, while the other two armies screened his movement, and then to turn south to the railroad. Hood countered by moving Stephen Lee's Confederates to Ezra Church crossroads, where he hoped to engage Howard. Once Howard's Federals were engaged, A. P. Stewart's Confederates, having taken another route to the same area, were to strike Howard on the flank, inflicting a decisive defeat. Unfortunately for Hood, the Federals were already there in strength and in a good defensive position. The ensuing battle lasted from early afternoon until dark, when the Confederates withdrew into the Atlanta fortifications. Hood had succeeded in keeping the railroad open, but at the cost of 5000 casualties to the Union's 600.

Still unable to cut off Atlanta, Sherman employed a new strategy. On August 9 he began a devastating, indiscriminate artillery bombardment of the city. Hood's response was to send Fighting Joe Wheeler's cavalry to raid the railroad between Atlanta and Chattanooga in hope of cutting Sherman's supply line. This proved ineffective, for Sherman had all the supplies he needed for the time being, the railroad was well guarded by Federal blockhouses at every bridge and Sherman's repair crews could lay down track as fast as Wheeler's men could tear it up.

Wheeler's raid, which lasted a month, was in fact a blunder, since the absence of cavalry left the Confederate defenses in a weakened position. On August 26 Sherman pulled Schofield's and Thomas' armies out of their trenches and marched them west around the city and then south toward the rail line. Hood misunderstood this to mean that Sherman had given up, and, after a brief celebration, Hood sent troops 15 miles south to Jonesboro to hasten Sherman's retreat. There the last battle for Atlanta was fought on August 31. The Federals easily repelled Hood's forces (Federal losses of 170 to Confederate's 1725) and cut the railroad in two places. Atlanta was now doomed.

Above: *General Sherman in a picture taken by the noted Civil War photographer Mathew B. Brady near Atlanta.*

Overleaf: *One of Sherman's cavalrymen examines a Rebel fortification north of the city of Atlanta.*

On September 1, 1864, Hood evacuated Atlanta, blowing up whatever supplies he could not carry away. Sherman marched in the next day, telegraphing Lincoln "Atlanta is ours and fairly won." Lincoln was overjoyed. Election day was two months away, and Sherman had just greatly improved his chances of winning.

Sherman pursued Hood southwest to Lovejoy, but when he found Hood's position too strong to assault, he ordered his troops back to Atlanta. While resting and regrouping in

A battery of the 5th US Artillery occupies a Rebel fort at Atlanta. General Sherman is visible in the background leaning against the parapet.

Above: *Part of the Confederate defenses of Atlanta. The elaborate fortifications were under continual bombardment by Sherman's forces.*

Atlanta, Sherman ordered the town's civilian evacuation. Defending this unpopular decision, he wrote to Halleck: "We want all the houses of Atlanta for military storage and occupation. We want to contract the lines of defense . . . . [This] will make it necessary to destroy the very houses used by families as residences . . . [and] to feed them or to see them starve under our eyes . . . . Families of our enemies would be a temptation and a means to keep up a correspondence dangerous and hurtful to our cause. These are my reasons; and, if satisfactory to the Government of the United States, it makes no difference whether it pleases General Hood and his people or not."

It did not please Hood. He and Sherman began a lengthy, heated correspondence not only over the evacuation but also over Sherman's earlier decision to shell Atlanta and her citizens. Sherman wrote back: "I was not bound by the laws of war to give notice of the shelling of Atlanta, a 'fortified town, with magazines, arsenals, foundries, and public stores;' you were bound to take notice. See the books." Between September 11 and 20, 1600 civilians were forced to abandon their homes and nearly all their possessions. Expecting cries of protest, Sherman wrote, "If the people raise

a howl against my barbarity and cruelty, I will answer that war is war and not popularity-seeking."

His popularity in the South certainly did not improve with his next course of action. Hood was on the move again; he had recaptured Allatoona and Dalton and was now trying to sever Sherman's supply lines. Realizing that he could not effectively engage Hood's army and hold Atlanta at the same time, Sherman decided to strike into the interior of the Confederacy.

Convincing Grant to accept this plan was easy. The two generals had an extended argument over Sherman's proposed march. Grant wanted Hood eliminated before Sherman went off on a new campaign. Sherman promised he would leave Thomas to deal with Hood, but Grant was not certain Thomas could handle him alone. Also, Grant felt the navy should capture a seaport city first, so that Sherman would have a supply base when he moved east.

Sherman seemed to be the only one who realized what a blow it would be to Southern morale, as well as resources, if the South proved unable to stop his march. He argued: "Until we can repopulate Georgia, it is useless to occupy it, but the utter destruction of its roads, houses and people will cripple their military resources . . . . I can make the march and make Georgia howl!" Grant replied, "On reflection, I think better of your proposition."

Now that the question of his march was settled, Sherman had to decide where he would go. The easiest route would be to the Gulf, burning cotton and freeing the prisoners at Andersonville on the way. On the other hand, he could probably destroy Hood if he went by way of the Chattahoochee River to Montgomery, Alabama, and then to the Gulf. But in the end, the march Sherman chose was to the sea at Savannah and then up the coast to help Grant finish Lee at Richmond.

Sherman sent Schofield's corps by train off to Nashville to help Thomas take care of Hood, Forrest and Wheeler (Forrest had just captured two gunboats and five transports on the Tennessee River), and in addition, Sherman also sent Thomas the bulk of his cavalry. Then he sent his excess supplies and his wounded by train to Chattanooga. Before the train left, he wrote Grant that, "I will not attempt to send couriers back, but trust to the Richmond papers to keep you well advised."

A week after Lincoln was re-elected president, Sherman cut loose from his supply lines and left Atlanta in flames: to have left it otherwise would be the same as handing it back to Hood. The factories would have recommenced producing needed supplies for the Confederate armies, and the railroads would have again begun moving the troops. So Sherman had ordered the destruction of factories, warehouses, railroad installations and any property Hood might find useful. Recalling the destruction of the railroads, Sherman wrote: "The whole horizon was lurid with the bonfires of rail ties, and groups of men all night were carrying the heated rails to the nearest trees and bending them around the trunks."

His engineer corps may have overstepped his orders in their fervent efforts to clear Atlanta. If so, it would not be the last time.

Above: *Sherman's men tearing up rail lines in Atlanta. The heated tracks would be bent around trees to prevent any possibility of reuse by the Rebels.*

Below: *Under the new concept of total war, prison camps such as Andersonville (Ga.) were set up. Some 50,000 men died in these camps.*

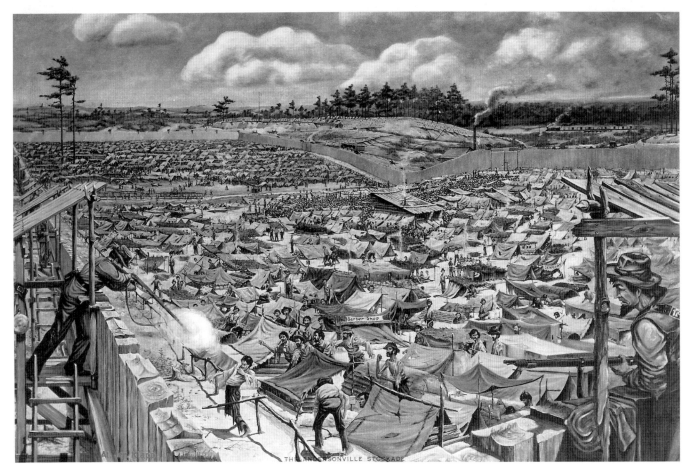

The March to the Sea

General Sherman left Atlanta at seven in the morning, November 16, 1864, astride his blaze-faced horse Sam. His face was drawn with fatigue from the nightlong effort of fighting to save private homes from spreading fires. He lowered his formless black hat almost to his red beard after he turned back from looking at the 200 acres of ashes that had once been Atlanta. Behind him were 62,000 fighting men, each with only a blanket wrapped in a rubber poncho, a haversack, a tin cup, a musket and 40 rounds of ammunition.

This unprecedented march would make Sherman one of the most famous generals in history. He was now the supreme commander, alone and at large in the field. By ordering the telegraph lines cut and the railroads torn up until they reached the Atlantic, Sherman had severed all communications with the North. As Lincoln put it, "I know what hole he went in at," and that was all he would know until Sherman emerged from the hole on the Atlantic coast.

To confuse the enemy, he split his army into two wings. The left, under Henry Slocum, pointed toward Augusta, and the right, under Howard, headed toward Macon. Neither of these towns would be stormed. He had told Admiral David Porter to expect the army to appear on the coast somewhere between Savannah and Hilton Head around Christ-

mas. His army, marching ten miles a day, was spread across a wide front of 60 miles, for Sherman's troops would need to scour a wide area if they were to keep from starving.

It was not, however, to be a free-for-all. Sherman's orders were to forage liberally, but he forbade trespassing in dwellings or using abusive or threatening language, and the soldiers were to leave families with enough food for sustenance. Only in areas of guerrilla activity were the men to burn and devastate. Alas, not everyone would obey his orders.

In his memoirs Sherman gives an example of a daily forage: "Each brigade commander had authority to detail a company of foragers, usually about fifty men, with one or

Below: *General Sherman and his senior officers. Left to right: Oliver O. Howard, Hugh Judson Kilpatrick, John A. Logan, William B. Hazen, General Sherman, Jefferson C. Davis, Henry Slocum, Francis P. Blair and Joseph A. Mower.*

Right: *General Hugh Judson Kilpatrick commanded the cavalry in Sherman's army.*

Right below: *In a Thomas Nast drawing for* Harper's *US soldiers rest on their march across the South.*

two commissioned officers selected for their boldness and enterprise. This party would be dispatched before daylight . . . and visit every plantation and farm within range. They would usually procure a wagon or family carriage, load it with bacon, corn-meal, turkeys, chickens, ducks, and every-thing that could be used as food or forage . . . [and] they would deliver to the brigade commissary the supplies . . . . No doubt, many acts of pillage, robbery, and violence, were committed by these parties of foragers, usually called 'bummers'; for I have since heard of jewelry taken from women, and the plunder of articles that never reached the commissary; but these acts were exceptional and inciden-tal. I never heard of any cases of murder or rape; and no army could have carried along sufficient food and forage for a march of three hundred miles; so that foraging in some shape was necessary."

Some of the soldiers roamed the counryside far from their units. (If, however, they wandered too far, Wheeler was there to pick off stragglers.) They took what they wanted, and when they were able to carry no more, they destroyed the rest. In fact, the army had more food than it could use. Fall harvest had left Georgis fat, but Sherman's men reversed that. Excess food was left along the road to spoil. As one officer put it: "Our men are clear discouraged with foraging, they can't carry half the hogs and potatoes they find right along the road."

Besides the sanctioned foragers and other soldiers, Sher-man's army was followed by the even more destructive and lawless band called "bummers." Composed of deserters

Right: *On his march through Georgia, General Sherman ordered telegraph lines cut and railroads torn up until he reached the Atlantic.*

from both Federal and Confederate armies, these men pillaged, burned and raped their way to the coast completely out of control.

Some Southerners were luckier than others. One elderly woman buried the family's valuables and watched Sherman march by. Another woman saw her recently deceased dog dug up four times. Still another woman, a native of Maine, pleaded for Federal guards to protect her property. She received guards, but they could not stop the pillagers, who came like a swarm of locusts, devouring everything in their path. In one case, Federal officers stopped at a farm and demanded to be fed. The meal was so delicious that they kidnapped the cook, though she managed to escape after tumbling from a mule. Contrary to what Sherman wrote in his memoirs, he once admitted in a speech that two cases of rape were brought to his attention. Southerners claim that rape was common but rarely reported by victims. As intended, Sherman's march gave Southern women a taste of the miseries of war.

Years later he would be credited with coining the phrase "war is hell." Actually, when he spoke to a crowd on August 11, 1880, at Columbus, Ohio, he said: "There is many a boy here today who looks on war as all glory, but, boys, it is all hell." The newspapers took the liberty of shortening it to "war is hell." There were not many Southern women living along his path who would disagree either way.

As with the bummers, thousands of Negroes, many of them women and children, followed the marching army. While bivouacked in Covington, Georgia, Sherman walked over to a nearby plantation and asked an old, gray-haired Negro if he understood about the war. Satisfied with his response, Sherman said: "I then explained to him that we wanted the slaves to remain where they were, and not to load us down with useless mouths, which would eat up the food needed for our fighting-men; that our success was their assured freedom ... [but] if they followed us in swarms of old and young, feeble and helpless, it would simply load us down and cripple us in our great task."

The one battle of this campaign – really no more than a tragic skirmish – occurred on November 22 at Griswold-

ville, a few miles east of Macon. Roughly 3700 Georgia militiamen under the command of General P. J. Phillips, attacked a rear-guard detachment. The militiamen, mostly boys under 16 and old men who were untrained and poorly armed, faced a veteran force of 1500 armed with Spencer repeating rifles. (Many western boys threw away the issued muskets and for $48 bought Spencers.) Three times the Confederates charged vainly across open fields in long lines, and the Federals continued to fire until the ground was thick with bodies. When it was over Sherman's men walked the battlefield seeing to the needs of the wounded; it was only then that the veterans discovered they had fought children and gray-haired men. One of the wounded boys said they had not wanted to fight, but since Confederate General Joseph Wheeler had taken every Georgia male who could carry a gun, they had been literally forced to do so.

On December 3 Sherman entered Millen, only to discover that the Federal prisoners he hoped to find there had been moved. He ordered the town destroyed. In Millen he learned that Hardee was waiting in Savannah with his small Confederate force of 9000, including the survivors of the skirmish at Griswoldville. Confederate Lieutenant General Richard Taylor, son of the late President Zachary Taylor, after inspecting Hardee's defenses, telegraphed Robert E. Lee that Savannah could not be held and urged that Hardee join Beauregard in Charleston, South Carolina. Lee agreed, and General Beauregard ordered a bridge built across the Savannah River to facilitate the garrison's retreat. The rice straw bridge, built by thousands of Federal prisoners, slaves and Confederate troops, was out of sight of Sherman's army on the Ogeechee River, where it had been since the December 13 storming of Fort McAllister, the capture of which had reestablished contact with the Federal fleet.

From Fort McAllister Sherman prepared to take Savannah. To Confederate Hardee he wrote, "Should I be forced to assault ... I shall then feel justified in resorting to the harshest measures and shall make little effort to restrain my army." Following a landing on Hilton Head Island by a division of Negroes under Federal General John L. Foster, Sherman was rowed downriver to discuss plans to cut off Hardee's escape. While he was away, on December 20 the Confederate army began its retreat under cover of darkness and fog, while Sherman's men waited at the city limits for orders. Trying to return from Hilton Head, Sherman was delayed aboard the steamer *Harvest Moon* when it grounded on a mud bank, and by time he arrived, his troops were already settled in Savannah and Hardee was long gone.

To President Lincoln he wrote: "I beg to present to you as a Christmas gift the city of Savannah, with one hundred fifty guns and plenty of ammunition, also about twenty-five thousand bales of cotton." Lincoln's reply was: "Many, many thanks for your Christmas gift. When you were about to leave Atlanta for the Atlantic coast, I was anxious, if not fearful, but feeling you were the better judge . . . I did not interfere. Now the undertaking being a success, the honor is all yours . . . But what next? I suppose it will be safe if I leave General Grant and yourself to decide."

Sherman had no sooner reached his headquarters in one of the town's most fashionable homes than he was inundated by civilians with requests for protection. Among them was General Hardee's brother with a letter from the general. To Ellen, Sherman wrote: "The three chief officers of the Rebel Army fled across the Savannah River, consigning their families to my special care." He did take care of these families and of many other destitute civilians, giving them army rations and over 50,000 bushels of captured rice.

Overnight Sherman had become a hero to the North; so much so that the usually critical press was now praising Sherman at the expense of Grant. Editors now called Grant an unimaginative officer who idled away his time near Lee's Richmond while Sherman slashed through the Deep South. Sherman was quick to defend Grant, saying: "General Grant is a great general. I know him well. He stood by me when I was crazy, and I stood by him when he was drunk; and now, sir, we stand by each other always."

Then amid the praise came the charge that he had allowed two Confederate armies to escape and had shown no concern for the plight of the Negroes. Charges that General Jefferson C. Davis (a Federal officer under Sherman, not to be confused with his namesake, the Confederate president) had abandoned black refugees at a stream crossing prompted this accusation. Though Sherman did have certain anti-black prejudices common to the time, he protested, saying: "Because I had not loaded down my army by the hundred of thousands of poor Negroes, I was con-

Above: *The Confederate army evacuating Savannah across a pontoon bridge under cover of fog and darkness on the night of December 20, 1864.*

Left: *Celebratory painting of Sherman and his generals at Savannah.*

strued by others to be hostile to the black race." But he steadfastly refused to enlist black regiments, which he believed Northerners favored "not from love of the Negro, but from a desire to avoid service."

Secretary of War Stanton arrived in Savannah to settle the issue. Sherman welcomed him, especially after having received a letter from John Sherman saying: "I live next door to Stanton, and he favors me with the dispatches when they

come. By the way, he is your fast friend, and was when you had fewer." Sherman welcomed the secretary, though he was somewhat nettled when Stanton asked a gathering of Negro clergy their opinion of the general. Hearing only praise for Sherman, Stanton then requested the general to design a plan to care for the former slaves. The plan, which was to be repealed during Reconstruction, called for the two rice field islands south of Charleston to be given to the

freed slaves. Each family would receive 40 acres of land and needed supplies.

After a month of city life, Sherman was ready to resume the march. "I was quite impatient to get off to myself, for city life had become dull and tame, and we were all anxious to get into the pine woods again." It had been nearly four years since South Carolina seceded, and the army itched to teach her a lesson.

Left: *View of the Savannah River at Savannah, a major port and supply depot for the Confederate forces.*

Above: *Edwin M. Stanton, Lincoln's secretary of war, favored the abolition of slavery and the military recruitment of blacks.*

Below: *A contemporary cartoon showing General Sherman as Santa Claus about to put the city of Savannah into Uncle Sam's stocking.*

FRANK LESLIE'S ILLUSTRATED NEWSPAPER.

The Final Campaign

Ten days before the fall of Savannah troops under General Thomas destroyed Hood's Confederate forces in the West. With the Confederate Army of Tennessee shattered, the only Confederate forces left to be reckoned with were Lee's 55,000 in Virginia and Beauregard's 17,000 in the Carolinas. Grant and Lee were in a stalemate, and, now that Sherman had finished his campaign, Grant urged him to come north to help in a joint effort against Lee. The joint venture would prove unnecessary.

Shortly after the beginning of the new year Sherman shipped Howard's right wing to Beaufort, South Carolina, where it would drive inland, outflank the Confederates and appear to be threatening Charleston. General Henry Slocum's left wing pushed slowly inland on each side of the Savannah River as if threatening Augusta. (Incessant rains flooded the southern portion of South Carolina, causing Slocum to wait ten days for the roads to dry.) Slocum's left wing would pass through Blackville, Lexington and Winnsboro before crossing into North Carolina and occupying Fayetteville. Howard would drive through Pocotaligo, Orangeburg, Columbia and Cheraw, then rendezvous with Slocum in Fayetteville.

Although this campaign was similar to the march to the sea, it was decidedly different in tone. South Carolina was the birthplace of secession, and while Sherman's soldiers had destroyed Georgia in the line of duty, here they acted with malice. Convinced that they would shatter the South's will to resist if they wreaked havoc on the first secessionists, the soldiers left nothing in their wake. They destroyed railroad tracks, stockpiles of ammunition, factories, mills, cotton and private property. As Sherman wrote from Savannah: "The whole army is burning with an insatiable desire to wreak vengeance upon South Carolina. I almost tremble at her fate, but feel that she deserves all that seems in store for her."

On January 21 Sherman sailed for Beaufort, South Carolina, to join Howard's command. He left General J. G. Foster in charge of the Savannah garrison, with orders to imprison any newspaper reporters who discovered the secret plan of the campaign. His newspaper image had improved briefly since he allowed reporters to accompany him on the march to the sea; perhaps they did not realize he allowed it only because he knew they would be unable to file their stories until the march was over. Nor were they within shouting distance when, before the Battle of Peachtree Creek, Sherman was informed of the apparent deaths of three of them. His gruff reply was something about having news from hell before breakfast.

As Sherman's two wings marched into South Carolina, Federal Brigadier General Hugh Judson Kilpatrick's cavalry spurred toward Augusta. Not knowing where the Federal army was going, Beauregard tried to garrison both Augusta and Charleston. Confederate General Joe Wheeler's cavalry fell back steadily as Sherman marched deeper into South Carolina. He hoped to catch the Federal troops bogged down and exposed in the swamps, but the swamplands did not prove to be a major obstacle to Sherman's hardy men as the Confederates had hoped. Although at times the troops struggled to achieve two miles a day, they averaged 13. The Western men slept standing in water when necessary; wounds that would have sent Sherman's command of East-

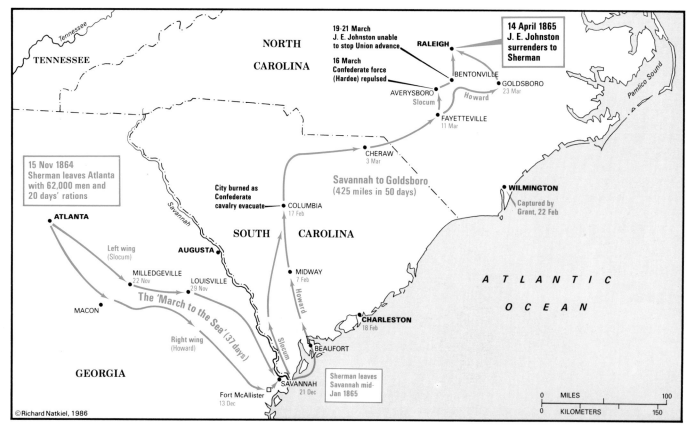

ern volunteers at Bull Run to the hospital were laughed off by these men. It was not unusual to find headquarters high in a tree, with the corps commander perched in the crotch. Sherman himself shrugged off the offer of a rug as he lay on a hard church pew one stormy night.

Although the Federal marchers were forced to deal with almost constant skirmishing, the first real resistance in South Carolina, and the last, met Howard's wing. Confederate General William Hardee set up an ambush with some 10,000 soldiers straegically placed along the flooded Salkehatchie River, the first great barrier in Howard's path. For three days Hardee's men fired on the Federal troops as the Westerners forced their way through the marsh. Union divisions under Generals Joe Mower and Giles A. Smith were diverted to deal with Hardee. Though under fire, the Federals had to suspend their cartridge boxes from the muzzles of their guns or fasten them around their necks to keep the powder dry. They placed diaries, money and other valuables in their hats as the water reached their armpits. The swamp was littered with wounded Federals from Mower's and Smith's divisions, groaning and dying. Some drowned as they slipped wounded into the water. But after three

Above: *Sherman oversees the artillery bombardment in the siege of Atlanta in August 1864.*

Right: *General Sherman's temporary headquarters in the pine woods. In the wet swamplands of South Carolina, corps headquarters might sometimes be in a tree.*

Left: *Map of Sherman's march to the sea and the movements of Howard and Slocum in South Carolina and North Carolina, ending on April 14, 1865, with General Johnston's surrender to Sherman at Raleigh.*

Right: *To destroy a railroad, raiders on both sides would often stack the crossties, lay the torn-up rails at an angle over them and set the wood afire. The heated rails would bend out of shape by their own weight.*

Below: *Sherman's men moving through the marshlands of South Carolina, February 1, 1865.*

hours the Federals reached the far shore, where Hardee's men were beginning to pull back. When a flanking Federal column crossed upstream at Beaufort's Bridge, the surprised enemy was routed "in utter disorder," as Sherman wrote in his memoirs.

Meanwhile, Sherman's main body was laying crude roads for the wagons. After that the Federals crossed the flooded Salkehatchie with wagons and guns in two days. When General Joseph E. Johnston, who would have the dubious honor of being restored as the commander of the Confederate forces in the Carolinas on February 23, heard of Sherman's speedy crossing, he said: "I made up my mind that there had been no such army in existence since the days of Julius Caesar."

On February 16 Sherman was in sight of the flaming bridge over the Broad River opposite Columbia. That night he, along with many of his regiments, slept at Camp Sorghum, an abandoned prison with space for 500 that had

been filled with 13,000 captured Federal officers. Although the officers had been shipped out in cattle cars the previous day, a few escapees told Sherman and his troops about their plight. (One of the prisoners was Captain S. H. M. Byers, who wrote a popular song about Sherman's march to the sea that managed to find its way into a Northern newspaper. Sherman attached him to his staff as a reward.) The Union troops' affection for Columbia did not increase when they heard the prisoners' tales of horror.

As the last of Confederate General Wade Hampton's cavalrymen were riding out of town, Colonel George A. Stone's brigade of Iowa men marched in. Sherman had ordered that only war materials and public buildings were to be burned, but, either the Confederate cavalrymen upon leaving, or the Federal soldiers upon entering, set fire to the cotton that had been stacked in the streets. High winds spread the fire, and before it was over two-thirds of South Carolina's capital was burned to the ground.

When, on March 7, Sherman pressed into North Carolina, he issued orders for milder treatment of that state, saying: "Deal as moderately and fairly by North Carolinians as possible, and fan the flame of discord already subsisting between them and their proud cousins of South Carolina. There never was much love between them." But while few towns suffered, more timber was blackened thanks to the bummers following Sherman's army. The heavy smoke hung over the army, choking it. Even so, the tattered men, many of whom marched barefooted, were exuberant. The soldiers in the ranks cheered whenever Sherman went by. They realized how much their "Uncle Billy" had accomplished with so little bloodshed.

Filled with pride after his Westerners covered the last 15 muddy miles in five hours, Sherman arrived in Fayetteville on March 12. Confederate General Wade Hampton was amazed by his appearance and hurried from his breakfast table in order to get out of town. Sherman then spent two days preparing for what he was confident would be the last campaign of the war.

On March 18 Johnston's whole army hit Slocum's left wing at Bentonville. Sherman quickly sent reinforcements. The Fifteenth Corps marched all night to reach Slocum by dawn, and the Seventeenth Corps was right behind. The tide turned, and the Federals took the offensive. But when informed that Johnston had 400,000 men, Sherman waited until the approaching commands under Generals Schofield and Alfred H. Terry, which had just secured Fort Fisher – the last Confederate controlled major Atlantic seaport – could arrive. In the meantime, Mower attacked when he saw an opportunity to turn Johnston's flank. He was cutting through the surprised Confederate lines when Sherman ordered a halt, and Johnston slipped away. Sherman had missed his last chance for a great battle. Years later he would admit that he had made a mistake, but by then he knew that Johnston had not, after all, been 40,000 strong.

He found Schofield waiting with his corps in Goldsboro, and he met Terry and his 10,000 men at the edge of town. (This would not be the last time Terry would arrive a day late. In 1876 he would reach the Little Bighorn in time to bury five troops of his cavalry, which had been under the command of George Armstrong Custer.) Sherman was now 80,000 strong, and the campaign was over. Although he had never won a decisive battle, neither had he ever lost a campaign.

Leaving Schofield in command, Sherman traveled to City Point, where, on March 27, he met with Grant, Admiral Porter and President Lincoln on the steamer *River Queen.* Of his conversation with Lincoln, Sherman would writ in his memoirs: "Mr. Lincoln was full and frank in his conversation, assuring me that in his mind he was all ready for the civil reorganization of affairs at the South as soon as the war was over; and he distinctly authorized me to assure Governor Vance and the people of North Carolina that, as

Left: *General Sherman at the head of a column of troops entering Columbia, capital of South Carolina, February 17, 1865. By March 7 he was in North Carolina.*

Left: *President Lincoln with his top military commanders in 1865. General Sherman is standing behind him to his right; Grant is on his left.*

Above: *A Union assault on the defenses at Petersburg. Such attacks proved costly to Grant, who finally laid siege to the city.*

soon as the rebel armies laid down their arms, and resumed their civil pursuits, they would at once be guaranteed all their rights as citizens of a common country; and that to avoid anarchy the State governments then in existence, with their civil functionaries, would be recognized by him as the government de facto till Congress could provide others." Admiral Porter remembered Lincoln saying that he wanted peace on almost any terms. "His heart was tenderness throughout," Porter reflected, "and as long as the rebels laid down their arms, he did not care how it was done." Both Porter and Sherman heard him ask if it were possible to avoid another fight, for he wanted no more bloodshed. Grant and Sherman both told him that to end the war there would have to be "one more desperate and bloody battle." Sherman later said of Lincoln: "Of all the men I ever met, he seemed to possess more of the elements of greatness, combined with goodness, than any other."

On April 2 Lee withdrew his army from Petersburg, ending the six-months' siege, and Federal troops entered Petersburg and Richmond the next day. On April 5 President Lincoln toured Richmond, where he took great pleasure in sitting in Jefferson Davis' chair. Three days later Lee surrendered to Grant at Appomattox Court House, Virginia. The terms were: Confederate officers and men were free to return home with their horses, if they were privately owned, and the officers would retain sidearms; all other equipment was to be surrendered.

Eight days after Lee's surrender on April 17, 1865, General Johnston met Sherman at a little farmhouse known as Bennett Place near Durham, North Carolina, to negotiate surrender terms. Sherman had been handed a coded dispatch just as he was boarding the train at Raleigh for the trip to Durham. The message was from Stanton, announcing the assassination of President Lincoln. Fearing violent retaliation by his men, Sherman said nothing about it until he was alone with Johnston. The Confederate general read the telegram with great distress, knowing it to be "the greatest possible calamity to the South." Sherman offered the same terms of surrender that Grant had given Lee. Johnston promised to get President Davis' approval for the surrender of all the Confederate armies and to return the next day.

When they met the next day Johnston had with him the Confederate Secretary of War, Major General John Breckenridge, who told Sherman of the uneasiness of the Southern officers and soldiers about their political rights. Having been told by Lincoln to accept any terms, Sherman sat down and wrote out terms that included Southerner's political rights. Satisfied, Johnston and Breckenridge signed the agreement.

Secretary of War Edwin Stanton, who, had assumed the reins of command in the wake of Lincoln's death, rejected the agreement. Believing the Confederacy was responsible for Lincoln's assassination and fearing Sherman had designs for a dictatorship (a nonsensical fear in view of the fact that Sherman, when asked a year earlier to run for office, had said that he would rather be in the penitentiary) told newspapers that Sherman had willfully disobeyed Lincoln's order of March 3 directing Grant to hold no conferences with the enemy on political questions. (Sherman had not seen the order.) Stanton fed more half-truths to the newspapers until Sherman's image as a hero had all but vanished. The *New York Herald* wrote: "Sherman's splendid military career is ended, he will retire under a cloud . . . with a few unlucky strokes of his pen, he has blurred all the triumphs of his sword."

Sherman was outraged, not only at Stanton, but at Halleck for siding with him. He knew that Lincoln had wanted a hard war but a soft peace. But on April 26, 1865, with Grant at Sherman's headquarters in Raleigh giving support, Sherman returned to Bennett's farmhouse, where he offered Johnston the same terms of surrender that were given to Lee. Johnston agreed with hesitation.

General Sherman intended to tell his side later before the War Investigating Committee, but when, on May 22, he realized that the committee was eager to prove Lincoln's policy of mercy had been a mistake, he changed his mind.

He and Grant remained silent as to what President Lincoln had said to them on the *River Queen.* Only in his memoirs did Sherman set the record straight.

Both Sherman and General Johnston found the path to peace less than smooth. Confederate President Davis blamed Johnston for his capture because the general would not give him a calvary detachment. Johnston could not, for he was honor bound to the surrender terms. Because of the personal attacks on Sherman, his army was looked down upon by the Army of the Potomac. It took Grant's order to get the Western army into Washington for the review on May 24, 1865. If Sherman had given the order, his men would probably have taken up arms against the Easterners. Instead, they showed up the Army of the Potomac, which had marched poorly in review on May 23, by marching the following day as if they had been born to parade. Sherman observed, "I believe it was the happiest and most satisfactory moment of my life." As he passed the review stand Sherman whipped out his sword and saluted the President. The crowd cheered; Sherman was still a hero.

Below: *At Bentonville, North Carolina, Confederate and Union forces engaged in the last orderly battle of the war, Less than a month later Sherman accepted Johnston's surrender.*

Right: *Above a depiction of the assassination of Lincoln three weeks earlier, this New York newspaper ran an editorial highly critical of the surrender terms that Sherman offered to Johnston.*

96

29, 18

FRANK LESLIE'S
ILLUSTRATED
NEWSPAPER

Entered according to the Act of Congress in the year 1864, by FRANK LESLIE, in the Clerk's Office of the District Court for the Southern District of New York.

O. 501—VOL. XX.]   NEW YORK, MAY 6, 1865.   [PRICE 10 CENTS. $4 00 YEARLY. 12 WEEKS $1 00.

Alas, Sherman!

AMONG the men whom the nation delighted (and still delights) to honor was and is Gen. Sherman, the brilliant Marshal of the calm, flexible and trenchant Grant—whose wide generosity has always overflowed towards his subordinates, and is as grand as his own subordination to the lawful authorities of the country is conspicuous. As Lieutenant-General of the armies of the United States, he held parliamentary intercourse with the General commanding the forces of the rebellion, but he did so in the purest military sense. He never undertook to compromise the nation.

He frankly told the chief in arms of the most gigantic Treason the world ever saw, that he had no office beyond that of soldier in the field. He undertook no adjustment of questions outside of the soldier's province. He said in words that will live among the most memorable in History, when proposing terms of capitulation to Lee, "I regard it as my duty to shift from myself the responsibility of any further effusion of blood, by asking you to surrender." He revolved within his own sphere. He did precisely what was within his duty and authority to do. He did not undertake to dictate, even by implication, the policy of the country, but

told the subtle rebel commander, who vainly sought to entrap his liberal and generous spirit, by making the surrender of his army the condition of amnesty to traitors, that "the terms upon which peace could be had were well understood," and these were "by laying down their arms" and submitting to the authority of the nation. Mark: the first General of the United States was then dealing with the first General of the rebellion; in a military sense these were the two pre-eminent men in this terrible conflict. Grant acted purely within his line of duty and scope of power.

But what happens now? A Lieutenant

subordinate, a brilliant and justly successful General within his range of duty, but who had nothing more to do with the planning of the great campaign that has terminated successfully than dozens of others, has undertaken to settle all the great questions to which that struggle has given rise. Neither Heaven or earth ever witnessed a presumption equal to this! What authority or right had Johnston, the wretched, hundred-times beaten Johnston, who had not a single soldier ready or willing to use arms in support of a fallen cause, and who himself could not count upon a dozen followers to help save him from a well-earned

The Later Years

If the newspapers thought they had lost one of their favorite targets, they must have been relieved to find that Sherman was not yet ready to fade into political or military obscurity. Within weeks of the end of the war Sherman was assigned by the US Army to St. Louis to oversee and protect the next great challenge that Americans were undertaking. For him, building the transcontinental railroad and sub-

duing the Plains Indians would now replace destroying the Southern railroads and emancipating the Negroes.

As commander of the Division of the Mississippi, Sherman put the resources of the army into building the transcontinental railroad. His troops guarded the railroad crews, many of his former officers were executives with the line and hundreds of his former soldiers men who had become

adept at twisting rails now laid them. Sherman could not ride down the line without hearing cheers for "Uncle Billy."

The newspapers may have missed a chance when Sherman, no doubt in jest, said that the United States ought to declare war on Old Mexico and make it take back New Mexico. But they readily crucified him when, after the Custer debacle, he was prompted to tell Grant: "We must act with vindictive earnestness against the Sioux, even to their extermination, men, women, and children." This was translated in the papers as "Sherman is for exterminating Indians."

Left: *Sherman, now commander of the military division of the Mississippi, was given a rousing reception in the US House of Representatives on January 29, 1866.*

Above: *In full dress uniform, General William Tecumseh Sherman sits for his portrait in 1888, five years after his retirement as general-in-chief of the US Army.*

Sherman was actually sympathetic to the Indian cause. He was one of the first to see how the dwindling bison would cause the demise of the Plains Indians, as would the railroad he was helping to build. To Ellen, he wrote from Kansas: "The poor Indians are starving. We kill them if they attempt to hunt and if they keep within the Reservations they starve."

On November 7, 1868, U. S. Grant was elected president. When he was inaugurated on March 4, 1869, Sherman succeeded him as General of the Army, from which position he would retire on November 1, 1883. It would be the last time Sherman replaced Grant, even though every few years he was asked to run for the presidency. When, in 1884, he received a telegram for a delegate at one of the political conventions saying he was being nominated, Sherman wired back, "I will not accept if nominated and will not serve if elected."

Believing he had no real authority over military matters, Sherman had moved both his office and family to St. Louis in 1874, but he returned to Washington two years later when he received General Order No. 28 returning all military control to the General of the Army. "This is all I had ever asked," Sherman wrote in his memoirs.

While he was in St. Louis his duties had been so slight that he had time to write his memoirs. He said he intended them as a lesson in obeying federal laws, but the memoirs, published shortly after, would not be read as he envisioned. Instead, his words had the effect of pouring salt on the wounds of Southerners, drew criticism from Northerners, alienated friends and provoked petty charges from former officers in the Army of the Cumberland of favoritism toward the Army of the Tennessee.

But if the controversial Sherman remained good newspaper copy to the last, he also remained a national hero. He spoke at hundreds of dinners, never asking for a fee, for he felt it his duty to instruct the younger generation in loyalty and obedience to federal law.

At home he was just plain Cump and deferred to Ellen on all family matters. He turned his paycheck over to her, and she made all household decisions. Once he mentioned that Grant wanted his son, Fred, and their son, Tom, to go to the same school; Ellen told him that either Tom was going to the Jesuit College at Georgetown or she would take them all back to her father. Sherman did not speak for days, but the boy went to Georgetown and later became a priest, without Sherman's blessing. When a relative tasted her coffee and found it too sweet, Ellen tartly told her to pass it on down to Cump, since he wouldn't notice.

He never turned away a former soldier in need. He estimated that a third of his salary went toward paying for train

The Battle of the Little Bighorn, in which Colonel George Armstrong Custer's 7th Cavalry Regiment was annihilated on June 25, 1876, by a large force of Sioux warriors, stirred considerable controversy over US indian policy.

tickets, boots and clothing for old comrades in arms, and he provided assistance to the widows and orphans of soldiers whenever asked. When the impoverished Grant was racing to finish his memoirs before cancer consumed him, it was Sherman who visited him most regularly. Sherman was offended that Grant's family, at his death on July 23, 1885, had allowed his body to be entombed in a huge mausoleum, and let it be known that he himself wanted to be buried in a less ostentatious fashion.

After he moved to New York in 1886 he was kept busy attending reunions and banquets (almost nightly). He also found himself, increasingly, attending the funerals of old colleagues. He wrote to Ellen in late 1888 that he would not attend any more burials of generals except his own. Nine weeks later he buried Ellen in St. Louis beside Willie and Charles.

On February 14, 1891, after a ten-day illness, William Tecumseh Sherman succumbed to asthma. Although he had requested that only his family see his remains, it was

Above left: *An 1869 poster announcing the opening of the Omaha to San Francisco route of the Union Pacific. Sherman favored railroad growth.*

Above: *General Sherman (third from left) meets with Indians at Fort Lamarie in 1868 in a successful effort to end Red Cloud's War.*

decided that veterans should not be denied that privilege. Thousands of mourners viewed his body dressed in his general's uniform with a yellow sash across the breast, his cap and sword at his side. As the flag-covered casket was carried from the house to be borne to St. Louis, General Oliver Howard called out the order on the cold day. Next to the hearse stood a horse with the general's saddle and his boots reversed in the stirrups. Behind the hearse, for blocks, were the carriages of President Harrison and hundreds of other dignitaries. The honorary pallbearers stood bareheaded. Sherman's son-in-law told the eldest pall-

bearer to put his hat back on before he caught cold, but the 82-year-old General Joe Johnston replied "If I were in his place and he were standing here in mine, he would not put on his hat." Ten days later the old Confederae would die of pneumonia.

Thirty thousand veterans marched in the procession, which wound through crowded, silent streets, and when the body was transferred to the train, crowds stood along the tracks. Father Tom read the service in a Catholic church in St. Louis before taking his father to his final resting place beside Ellen. The Thirteenth Regulars fired three volleys above the grave that overlooked the Mississippi River. Then a bugle blew the sad, beautiful notes of "Taps," a call that had originated in the Confederate Army.

Index